my life as a wannabe Balanced MOM

my life as a wannabe Balanced Mom

CRYSTAL ESCOBAR

PLAIN SIGHT PUBLISHING
An imprint of Cedar Fort, Inc.
Springville, Utah

ISBN 13: 978-1-4621-2318-6

Published by Plain Sight Publishing, an imprint of Cedar Fort, Inc.
2373 W. 700 S., Springville, UT 84663
Distributed by Cedar Fort, Inc., www.cedarfort.com

LIBRARY OF CONGRESS CATALOGING-IN-PUBLICATION DATA

Names: Escobar, Crystal, 1981- author.
Title: My life as a wannabe balanced mom / Crystal Escobar.
Description: Springville, UT : Plain Sight Publishing, an imprint of Cedar Fort, Inc., [2019] | Includes bibliographical references and index.
Identifiers: LCCN 2018051966 (print) | LCCN 2018060771 (ebook) | ISBN 9781462130030 (epub, pdf, mobi) | ISBN 9781462123186 (perfect bound : alk. paper)
Subjects: LCSH: Escobar, Crystal, 1981- | Women--Life skills guides. | Women--Conduct of life. | Self-realization in women.
Classification: LCC HQ2037 (ebook) | LCC HQ2037 .E83 2019 (print) | DDC 158--dc23
LC record available at https://lccn.loc.gov/2018051966

Cover design by Wes Wheeler

Edited by Jessica Pettit and Nicole Terry
Typeset by Kaitlin Barwick

Printed in the United States of America

10 9 8 7 6 5 4 3 2 1

Printed on acid-free paper

This book is dedicated to my husband, Sean, and
our four children, Lily, Oliver, Brooklyn, and Owen.
Because without YOU, I wouldn't be ME.

And to mothers everywhere who continue to seek
growth, inner truth, and enlightenment as they
strive to imperfectly raise perfect children.
May you find peace in your journey.

Contents

Introduction

Let's address the elephant in the room, shall we? I'm not always balanced. In fact, I'm really good at *not* being balanced.

In my quest for the cure-all idea of balance, I unwittingly opened the floodgates of personal development. I came face to face with the lies I had created in my mind over years of suppressing my true self, my inner being, my SOUL.

I found myself experiencing a full-on identity crisis—yes, the cliché midlife crisis that inevitably happens to the ones you least expect, the ones who on the outside look as though they have it all together. The truth is, I was falling apart internally.

Who am I really? was a question I could not quite answer. Am I living up to my potential? Am I loving with all my heart? Why am I so jealous, needy, and insecure? Why do I always feel so emotionally unstable? Perhaps I need medical attention, or maybe I'm just *craving* attention.

Analyzing my motives behind everything I've ever done, tracing it back to the core, I discovered something I wasn't too proud of. I unveiled my deep desire to be popular and admired—famous, even. I was desperate for approval, not realizing the betrayal I bestowed upon myself in an attempt to gain praise and recognition. I had been sacrificing the true part of me in pursuit of adoration and self-worth.

It was time for some soul searching.

Being a well-rounded person has always been a goal of mine. I remember that even as a young girl I would make to-do lists that always incorporated mind, body, and soul.

Read a book. Check.

Ride my bike around the block ten times. Check.

Surprise my mom by cleaning the house for her. Check.

It gave me a sense of accomplishment and pride as I checked off each task, feeling as though I had cracked the code to life. Oh, to be a naive ten-year-old again.

Now, fast forward to my life as a mom of four pushing forty. I've realized just how far I've come in my quest for balance. We all "wanna be" balanced, right?

Being balanced is like being perfect: ain't no mama got time for that.

I've spent most of my motherhood years checking things off my list, as if life were a mathematical equation. Mind + Body + Soul = Balance. If I do A, B, and C, then I'll be the perfectly balanced mom.

I would start my day with a prayer, read something inspirational, get on the treadmill, drink a protein shake, spend a little time developing a talent like learning the guitar, clean the house, play with my kids, make dinner, clean up, do laundry, bathe the kids, read them books, and then kiss them good night. Day after day after day I would follow this simple mechanical formula. I thought I would feel complete and balanced, like I was doing everything God has asked of me.

Instead my checked-off tasks felt completely futile and mundane. There was no passion or excitement. I needed a challenge, a purpose, a WHY. Let's be honest, the daily duties of a mother can seem quite monotonous at times. You cook, you clean, and you care for your child's every need. At the end of the day you're feeling physically exhausted and at the same time craving something more.

I didn't realize that my quest for feeling balanced and at peace would take much more than just mindlessly doing clear-cut tasks. It would take a lot more effort and brainpower to get to where I wanted to be.

The meaning of balance to me has changed substantially over the past decade. It has become more of a state of mind and less about my daily tasks. I finally discovered the missing link. The problem was that I didn't quite grasp the "mind" slice of balance. Now I understand that balance actually *starts* with the mind. A healthy mind breeds a healthy body and spirit.

I'm completely fascinated with how the mind works, the evolution of the brain, why we do what we do, the brain default settings, memory, decision-making, motivation, emotions, habits, neurotransmitters, and all things meditation, manifestation, and law of attraction.

When I was twenty-one, I served an eighteen-month Christian mission in Germany. I spent two months in a training center to help me learn the language and to prepare me for the work ahead. I remember looking up at the beautiful Provo mountains each morning as my partner and I walked to the cafeteria for breakfast. I once said to my partner, "Look how foggy the mountains are." She seemed confused and informed me that the mountains were in fact beautifully crisp.

It was at that moment that I realized I needed glasses. I had been going about my life not even knowing my vision was blurry. The next day I got glasses and instantly gained a different perspective. I could now SEE everything with a newfound sharpness.

As I've spent time studying the mind and doing the work required on my own brain, I've been able to operate more from positive emotions, as opposed to the regular negative emotions that seemed to cloud my perception. Suddenly I see things much more clearly. I understand now what was keeping me from feeling my best physically and being truly centered and connected to God. I realized that by feeding the negative emotions and believing the thoughts that were creating the emotions, I unintentionally constructed a barrier between God and me. God speaks to us through our spirits, and when our minds/egos are controlling the show, our spirits get stuck backstage hidings their gifts and talents from the audience.

It's amazing how a healthy mind can provide the focus needed to be led by your intuition as you work toward achieving goals.

Just five years ago, I wondered why I always seemed to have so much drama in my life. Why *did* so many negative emotions seem to fester within my soul? Resentment, jealousy, anger, boredom, discouragement, and shame seemed to be my constant companions. I thought, *I'm a nice person and a loyal friend. I take good care of my kids and do the right thing. How could any of these feelings be my fault?*

Everything seemed foggy. I believed others were *making* me feel the way I was feeling. I would get frustrated with people's lack of love and appreciation toward me. *How could they do this?* I thought.

When I finally put on my proverbial glasses, I began to see that my very own thoughts were the problem all along. I get to choose how I want to feel. When someone does something that hurts my feelings, it only hurts because of what I make it mean.

This piece of knowledge has literally set me free from all the internal torment I was experiencing. In this book, I will go into more detail and share personal experiences about times when I was overcome with resentment, jealousy, stress, and confusion. I've discovered the perfect remedy for every negative emotion and experience we are faced with in motherhood, and I'm looking forward to sharing it through my own personal story.

Chapter 1

I "Wanna Be" a Balanced Mom

In 2005, my daughter Lily Rea joined this world and officially made me a mom. I was overwhelmed with love and adoration. At the same time, I was overwhelmed with the hardest work I'd ever experienced. I finally understood what others said about motherhood being harder than a full-time job. It's literally 'round the clock work, and as a very sleep-deprived mom, I found myself experiencing the "baby blues." Being a first-time mom was a bit of a shock. Suddenly, my life was no longer my own. Baby girl owned me!

My season of motherhood had just begun, and I was already daydreaming of the day my kids would all be in school and I would have FREEDOM once again. I felt ashamed of these thoughts, as if there were something wrong with me. Why wasn't I fully enjoying the most sacred of all callings? Was I a selfish person for wanting time to myself?

A little time passed, and I got over my pity party and went to work. Like every new mother, I put my heart and soul into my child. I read baby books and wrestled with decisions. Co-sleeping or sleep training? Pacifiers or no pacifiers? Breast feeding or formula, cloth diapers or disposable diapers, schedule or no schedule? Should you wake a sleeping baby, or let the baby sleep?

I experienced the constant worry that whatever I did might be the wrong choice and that ten years down the road I would discover how badly I messed my child up—all because I gave her a bottle of formula.

In 2009, I had my second child, Oliver. When he was nine months old, I felt an overwhelming urge to start blogging. I followed the prompting and began my blog in 2010. It was a way for me to feel connected to the outside world and share my thoughts and life experiences. I discovered a community of other mothers just like me, feeling the very same feelings I had. I loved the process of vulnerably sharing real-life experiences. It was therapeutic in a way, giving me a release, an outlet I hadn't yet experienced as a mom.

I first titled my blog "Balanced Moms | Managing Life as a Mom." I wanted to attract a community of like-minded women, women who were also seeking balance and purpose in motherhood. I was extremely ~~obsessed~~ passionate about balance, or, in other words, PERFECTION. I was blogging about my quest for balance as a mom feeling the chaos of unpredictable days and never-ending to-do lists.

As a blogger, I was in love with my newfound hobby but always felt somewhat guilty for taking the time to work on it. I wanted to be the "perfect" mom, and my idea of the perfect mom was someone who selflessly gave ALL of her time to her family, leaving no room for herself.

So in my attempt to do both—be "the perfect mother" and continue blogging—I traded sleep for time to work on my blog. I felt completely scattered all the time. I wanted to have a balance but really had no clue how to obtain it. So I became the "Wannabe Balanced Mom."

The creative juices were in full flow. The more I pursued balance, the more ideas came to me, and the more I kept piling on. It wasn't long until the burnout happened. I lasted two years running this rat race, staying up late into the night to work on my projects. There were a million things I wanted to do. I wanted to write a book, create a day planner for moms, have an online boutique for girls, and learn to play the guitar and write a song. I was producing YouTube videos, writing blog posts, constructing meal plans, learning photography, reading self-help books, and planning creative crafts and activities to do with my kids, all while keeping my house spotless, making meals, scrapbooking, going to the gym, doing laundry, grocery shopping . . . Must I go on? You all know what I'm talking about.

The more I did, the more anxious I became. I would wake up every day feeling a weight on my shoulders. Finally, I realized that my blog about balance had triggered something in me that set me completely *off* balance. I was fooling myself into thinking I could do as much as I was doing and maintain a healthy balance.

I never thought there was such thing as being *too* ambitious. Now I know there is. As my life coach, Jody Moore, says, "Weaknesses are just strengths overused."[1]

Soon after I became a mom, I stumbled upon a humorous poem by Vickie Gunther that puts it perfectly:

The Perfect Woman

By Vickie Gunther

Look at me, look at me, look at me now.
You can do what I do, if you knew how!
I study the scriptures one hour each day;
I bake and upholster and scrub, and I pray.

She goes on to list a million other things this "perfect" woman was able to accomplish each day and each year, putting all us regular mamas to shame, including the fact that her kids get straight As, her house is always clean, and she never forgets to get all done up for her hubby. Oh, and of course she also runs a successful home-based business, makes everything from scratch, and never yells at her kids.

> These things are not hard; it's good if you do them.
> You can if you try. Set your goals and pursue them.
> It's easy to do all the things that I do.
> If you plan and work smart, you can do them all too!
> "It's easy!" she said . . . and then she dropped dead.[2]

The funny thing is, when I read this poem I immediately printed it out to use as a guideline for my quest to become the PERFECT mom. Instead of recognizing the message behind it, I saw it as the blueprint I'd been searching for. *People may think it's impossible to do all this and maintain sanity, but I'm going to do it all! WITHOUT dying.*

Or so I thought . . .

Over the years, as I attempted to fulfill every responsibility and worthwhile goal I had as a mom, I literally drove myself insane. Each time I tried to do everything perfectly, I crashed and burned—and each time, I picked myself up and tried to do it all over again. That's the definition of insanity (You know that, right?): doing the same thing over and over, expecting a different result.

It took me ten years to learn this lesson, but I think I'm finally catching on. I don't need to keep adding to my list. I don't need to do it all in one day or one month. I want to focus on ONE thing at a time and give it my all. Quality is more important than quantity. It's not healthy to try to do as many things as possible until I run myself into the ground.

As a new mom, I guess I couldn't define the difference between determination and obsession. To me, being laid back was laziness, contentment was idleness, removing things from my task list was quitting, and admitting I couldn't do it all was weakness. Needless to say, humility was something I needed to learn. And I did.

I quit my blog after two years of hustling like a madwoman. I let it all go completely, and it felt liberating.

I took that extra energy and went "all in" as a mom, with no hobbies and no side gig—just pure motherhood. At this point, I was pregnant with Brooklyn, my third, and I discovered a new ~~obsession~~ passion: natural living. I started researching natural birth, extended nursing, homeschool, and all things hippie life. I had a renewed sense of enthusiasm for my life as a mom, and I became a full-on "crunchy mom," as some call it.

It was a beautiful three years of homeschooling, home birth, and homemaking. Although it was amazing, eventually I burned out once again. I couldn't maintain everything I wanted to do as a homeschooling mom; I needed a break. As much as I didn't want to admit it, I needed time to do things for me. I had to surrender to the idea that it's okay to have hobbies and ambitions outside of motherhood. Self-care as a mom was something I didn't completely understand at first. It felt indulgent and selfish. But the truth was, without self-care, I was exhausted, frustrated, and overwhelmed. I began to understand that the best gift you can give your children is a mother who is rejuvenated, resilient, and radiates energy and love. And the only way to possess these things was for me to take time to be alone, read books, write in my journal, meditate, or even go get a massage once in a while.

After I had Owen, my fourth baby, I quit homeschooling. I'll explain more about that in chapter three. But I remember that when Owen was nine months old I began feeling anxious once again. I needed a project, a goal, something to work toward. I prayed and prayed for God to lead the way. I wanted to know how I could contribute more in the world. I needed a challenge, a new passion.

I began feasting on books. I discovered a newfound love for learning—and I was actually enjoying it instead of doing it to check off my list. As I read and discovered new truths, I couldn't help but want to share them. So I decided to start blogging once again, this time with a new approach. When I went back to blogging, I vowed to be more mindful of my purpose to contribute to positivity in the world. I wanted to share all the amazing new truths I was uncovering as I took the time to read, ponder, and apply them to my life.

It wasn't long until I fell into the same trap I found myself in when I first started my blog in 2010. I was overwhelmed with negative emotions that came from comparing myself to others, craving validation, stressing about the constant upkeep required for the blog, overplanning my days with to-dos, and feeling immense pressure to keep up with the "perfect woman" schedule. I didn't like what was happening to me.

With the help of holistic healers and life coaches, I was able to dig deep and unearth what was going on with me and why I kept repeating the same pattern. I found that true balance MUST start with the mind. You can't be connected to God, your inner being, or your intuition if your mind is not healthy, like I said in my introduction. I have put on my glasses and now I *see* what I was missing all along. I clearly understand what needs to happen in order to feel balanced. And it all starts with my mind. What am I thinking?

The key to *your* balanced life starts with your mind, too. Brooke Castillo, founder of The Life Coach School, encourages everyone to use what she calls the CTFAR model to discover where the problem lies.[3]

I had to learn to ask myself these questions:

- What is my **Circumstance**?
- What are my **Thoughts** about the circumstance?
- How does that make me **Feel**?
- What **Actions** do I take?
- What is my **Result**?

By taking the time to change my thoughts, I've discovered a whole new world full of peace, abundance, love, and acceptance. Like Byron Katie says in her book, *Loving What Is*, "When [you] argue with reality, [you] lose—but only 100 percent of the time."[4]

For me the circumstance was *I'm a mom.*

My thoughts were *I'm not supposed to have interests. I should be playing with and teaching my kids all day long. I'm selfish for wanting to pursue my hobbies. There's so much to do and not enough time. This is hard. I can't keep up. I should be doing more.*

These thoughts caused me to *feel unfulfilled, ashamed, overwhelmed, and resentful much of the time.*

My actions were to *stop pursuing my goals and hobbies but continue to add more to my plate in other ways.*

The result is that *I didn't show up as the kind of mother I wanted to be for my children. I wasn't rejuvenated, and often felt depleted and tired. My frustrations overflowed in the way I responded to my husband and children. I was not as sweet and patient as I knew I could be.*

As soon as I accepted that self-care was not selfish, I realized that it's actually essential for me to be the happy, energetic mother I wanted to be.

Just as flight attendants instruct us in the event of an emergency to put our air masks on first and then help our children, we as parents need to take care of ourselves because we are of no use to our children if we're not able to breathe.

> Find some time for yourself to cultivate your gifts and interests. Pick one or two things that you would like to learn or do that will enrich your life, and make time for them. Water cannot be drawn from an empty well, and if you are not setting aside a little time for what replenishes you, you will have less and less to give to others, even to your children.[5]

It's okay to do things you love. But like Elder Ballard said, choose ONE or TWO things, not five or ten. That's the key here. If I'm not careful, I can become overzealous and add too much to my plate. Changing my blog name to "Wannabe Balanced" was the most authentic way to describe myself. I "wanna be" balanced, I "wanna be" happy, I "wanna be" a good mom, I "wanna be" excited about life, and I "wanna be" amazing at all the things that are most important in my season of motherhood.

My new thoughts about balance:

- I have hobbies and interests and want to grow as a person.
- It's important I take time to do what replenishes me.
- I don't have to do it all.
- Everything I choose to do for my children and me is exactly the way it's supposed to be.
- I'm still a good mom even though I quit homeschooling.
- It's okay to hire help.

Balance encompasses the mind, body, and soul. It's not a to-do list; it's a state of mind. As I've adapted this thought-work exercise, I've seen huge improvements in my overall well-being and sense of balance. I've been able to remove the mom guilt and feel satisfied with doing less.

Notes

1. "Ep. 64. Strengths and Weaknesses," *Jody Moore: Coaching with LDS Values*, Oct. 7, 2016, https://jodymoore.com/64-strengths-weaknesses.

2. Vickie Gunther, "The Girl in a Whirl," as quoted at http://mormon momma.com/girl-whirl.
3. "Ep #26: The Self Coaching Model," *The Life Coach School Podcast*, Oct. 9, 2014, https://thelifecoachschool.com/26.
4. Byron Katie, *Loving What Is* (New York: Harmony Books, 2002), 2.
5. M. Russell Ballard, "Daughters of God," *Ensign*, May 2008, 108.

Chapter 2

Everyone Has a Story, and It Was Meant to Be Shared

I've had a secret goal to write a book for over fifteen years now. I say "secret" because at first, I never told anyone for fear of being judged or criticized by others. When an opportunity to write a book fell into my lap, I felt extremely inadequate. I thought, *Who am I to write a book?* I barely graduated high school and only went to two semesters of college. I'm not a doctor or even a certified life coach. I don't have a fancy education, MA, MBA, or PhD. But I realized one thing I do have is a story.

When I think of all the people who have taken part in who I am as a person, I realize just how much we need each other in this life. We cannot become the best version of ourselves without the help and influence of others. We need their encouragement, advice, authentic stories, validation, love, support, knowledge, and understanding.

That's why I felt compelled to start blogging and why I'm now bursting with excitement to be finally writing this book. I wanted to openly share the lessons I've learned in hopes that it may help someone else experiencing the same thing. I wanted to take my MESS and turn it into my MESSAGE. That's exactly how I would describe my blog and my purpose. I'm just a wannabe who is trying to be balanced, and often my life is just a big ol' fat mess.

I believe we are all influencers, especially if you use social media. We use it to share our talents, inspire others, teach what we know, and connect with friends and family.

In this generation, social media is such a big part of our lives, and I believe it is good in moderation. But really, we crave real-life connections and face-to-face communication. I use social media as a way to reach more people, but we must not forget the value of in-person connection.

My Story

Growing up for me came with a lot of dysfunction. *Turns out I wasn't the only one.* I have come to believe we all come from some sort of dysfunction. I used to be so ashamed of my family life. There was a lot that went on behind closed doors that I never wanted anyone to find out about. And it made for a very insecure little girl constantly afraid that the "secret" would get out and everyone would hate me and nobody would want to come play at my house. I had literal anxiety around this.

My mom had nine kids. Five of them had a different dad than me, but I always considered them my real brothers and sisters even though they didn't live with us for most of my growing-up years. We moved a lot and even lived in a tent in Hawaii for six months. Once I counted how many times we moved, and I lost track after twenty-five. It seemed like every six months we were packing up once again and I had to switch schools mid-school year. I was the eternal "new kid," and I always felt behind in school because of the adjustment period each time I switched curriculums. This feeling caused me to adopt the belief that I wasn't smart. I was always in the lowest reading levels and often ended up with the "special" group of kids that needed additional help separate from the rest of the class.

We were also extremely poor, and my parents couldn't afford to put me in any kind of extracurricular activities, like dance, piano, soccer, and so on. This gave me more "evidence" to support my belief that I wasn't good at anything. All my friends seemed to have a skill. I had no skills. No nunchuck skills or bowhunting skills . . . not even computer hacking skills. *Yes, I'm a fan of* Napoleon Dynamite.

As I got older and began hearing the stories of others, I found out that my home life was much more common than I ever realized. This released me from the bondage I had placed upon myself. Hearing other people's stories allowed me to say, "Me too," which does incredible things for the human spirit. Simply knowing that we are not alone, that we are understood, and that we can still be a part of the "tribe" is incredibly liberating.

I remember one Sunday at church when I was a young woman. My teacher was telling us how she met her husband. I was eager to hear her story because she seemed to have found her happily ever after, and I too wanted to find a good guy to marry one day. As part of the lesson she had us write down all the qualities we wanted in our future husband. Then she said, "Now go and BE that person you want to marry."

I took a little detour in becoming the kind of person I wanted to marry. Little by little, I began making choices that led me down a darker path. I got into a serious relationship that wasn't good for me, then after high school I moved to Arizona with my best friend. I began a life of FREEDOM, *or so I thought.* I no longer had rules. I was officially on my own to do whatever the heck I wanted. Which, in my mind, meant staying up late, sleeping in late, going to clubs, drinking myself sick, and doing other regretful things I'd rather not say. Before I knew it, I had become the opposite of what I wanted in a husband.

One of my roommates, who was also my best friend's older sister, was someone I truly admired and looked up to. She seemed to have her life together, and I was intrigued by her success in business and her motivation to do hard things, like running marathons. Her example inspired me to start taking action toward bigger things other than club hopping, hunting for the hottest guys, and working as a waitress just to pay my rent.

The lesson from my Sunday school class always stood out in my mind and reminded me of what I really wanted for my future. The boyfriend I started dating in high school turned into a three-year, off-and-on relationship. After only six months of dating him, I knew we needed to break up, but it took me three years to actually get up the courage to do it. I was afraid of being alone and never finding anyone else. I would break up with him, and the next day I would go back to what was familiar and comfortable. I didn't want to deal with the pain of saying goodbye to someone who had become such a big part of my life. I felt so weak and powerless. I couldn't understand why I wasn't able to just move on. Instead, I continued the torment by proving to myself that I was weak.

During this time of consistently breaking up and getting back together, I enrolled in Scottsdale Community College and began training to run a marathon. This was a huge stepping stone for me in discovering what I was capable of. It empowered me. I saw something in myself that I never knew existed, and I realized that I CAN do hard things! I didn't realize someone like me could actually do something extraordinary.

I finally found the strength to overcome my codependency and broke up with the boyfriend once and for all. I began cleaning up my life, and at that point had an overwhelming desire to do good. So I chose to devote eighteen months of my life to volunteer service for my church. At first, I was afraid to tell people of my aspiration for fear they would laugh and tell me there was no way someone like ME could fulfill an eighteen-month Christian service abroad. I held it in for a while and then little by little started testing the waters. I told my family, then a couple friends, and that's when it became real for me. Although I don't think anyone really took me seriously.

I remember being at a little get-together with some friends from high school when I mentioned the fact that I wanted to go on a mission. One of the girls literally began to laugh, but not in a hurtful sense—she genuinely thought I was joking.

I was extremely insecure about my worthiness and spirituality level. I remember when I started going back to church I thought everyone was looking at me, wondering why I was there. I doubt that was really the case; instead, those feelings were created from my own thoughts and insecurities.

I spent the next year working various temporary jobs, reading as much scripture as I could, and secluding myself from friends. Not because I didn't love them anymore, but because I had chosen to follow the rules of my church and no longer consume alcohol. I remember the last time I went to a club; it was about six months after I stopped drinking and began preparing for my eighteen-month service. My friends and I were all dancing and having a really good time. They were drinking and I wasn't. I remember feeling a bit of social pressure, like I should go ahead and join them. Just as I was about to order a drink, my friend said, *"Wow, Crystal, I love that you can have so much fun without drinking alcohol."*

It was then that I realized two things. I CAN have fun without alcohol, and my example matters.

One day as I was working one of my temporary jobs, I happened to be sitting next to a woman who had recently returned from her Christian service. This was unusual because back in 2001 it wasn't as common for girls to fulfill these types of services.

I asked her all about her experience and how she made the decision to go. Come to find out, her past was very similar past to my own. It was her STORY that finally gave me permission to believe I, too, could do this service, no matter my past. Everyone has the ability to start a new life, make amends, and clear their slate. The past had passed, and it doesn't have to mean anything about my present or what I wanted for my future.

Fulfilling that eighteen-month service was extremely tough. There were many times I wanted to give up and go home. But I knew that giving up would only give me proof that I couldn't do hard things, and I was determined to prove to myself that I was capable.

Like I said in the introduction, I was in the training center for two months, and it was the *longest two months of my life.* It was exceptionally hard being confined to such a small space, isolated from the outside world, knowing that everyone was going on with their lives while I was in there spending hours and days on end in a classroom, memorizing scriptures and learning the German language. It was overwhelming, to say the least.

I survived the two months, and then I was off to the airport to catch my first flight out of the country. At the airport we had permission to call our parents. I remember crying to my dad, afraid, overwhelmed, and even jealous of my friends and family who were home living their lives. My best friend had just gotten married, and I wasn't able to attend her wedding because I was in the training center. I, too, wanted to be home and getting married.

My dad assured me that this path was going to be an adventure worth taking and that I was lucky to get this experience before I got married. "You get to do both," he said. "You get to go on this mission AND get married." He reminded me of my long-term goals to grow as a person, overcome challenging things, and prepare myself to meet my future husband.

The personal growth that happened within those eighteen months was nothing short of a miracle. I remember my first couple weeks in Germany, overcome with jet lag, homesickness, and feeling completely ill equipped when it came to the language and my knowledge of the teachings.

As we bounced around the small city of Cottbus from one appointment to another, I remember struggling with the belief that I would ever learn the German language, let alone last the entire year and a half. I couldn't understand a word people were saying, and I struggled to stay awake during our meetings. I desperately wanted to give up and go home, but just as I was determined to prove to myself I could do hard things when I ran that marathon, this was something I was not about to quit. So I kept pushing through the difficulty and eventually found myself speaking German fluently and teaching lessons with confidence.

The last partner I worked with in Germany, Caeli Thibeault, was the one who inspired and encouraged me to write a book. She was an amazing writer. She had these huge journals and filled every page with the most beautiful and poetic words about her life and lessons she had learned. She made me feel smart even though she was, in my eyes, one of the smartest people I knew. She attended an Ivy League college and was so much further ahead than me academically and spiritually. But somehow, she helped me believe that I, too, had the potential to be smart and could even write a book someday.

Five months after I got home from Germany, I met the most amazing man, Sean Escobar. He was extremely good looking, charming, successful, and charismatic. I knew immediately he was the one for me. I had never in my life been treated with so much respect and adoration from a guy. One thing that really stood out for me was the fact that he *always* opened my door for me. Sounds kind of silly that it was such a big deal for me, but this was just something I always wanted from guys I dated, and surprisingly, not many practiced such chivalry.

The day after our first date, Sean, being the sweet and thoughtful man that he is, showed up on my doorstep with a bouquet of flowers and a little note. From that point on, we were practically inseparable.

Three months later we were married. *This, of course, caused people concern for the outcome of our marriage.* Not long after being married, I rediscovered the list I made back in Sunday school, the one that stated all the qualities I wanted in my future husband. Guess what? Sean had every single one of those qualities—and then some.

About a year into our marriage, I became a mom, and trying to manage my new life is what inspired me to start blogging about balance. I read other blogs as well. One blogger that stands out in my mind is Ree Drummond from *The Pioneer Woman*. I wanted to be just like her. She shared the most beautiful pictures of farm life as a homeschooling mom, she's an amazing photographer, and she's a talented chef. Everything she did was outstanding, and she inspired me in so many ways.

Michelle Duggar from the reality show *19 Kids and Counting* was another person who inspired me. I read her book and thought, *Wow, she has nineteen kids, she homeschools them all, AND she even wrote a book.* Can one possibly be any more amazing than that?

When I was pregnant with Brooklyn (my third), I watched a documentary directed by Abby Epstein called *The Business of Being Born*. I was sold on the idea, and home birth became my next endeavor.

I always had healthy pregnancies and healthy babies until my fourth baby, Owen. Right after delivering him in my bathtub at home, I was relishing in the beauty of the moment and the perfection of his tiny little body, when suddenly I noticed his ear didn't look quite right. It was a lot smaller than the other one and wasn't shaped like a normal ear. I immediately began thinking over my entire pregnancy, wondering what I must have done to cause this birth defect. What did I eat, drink, and breathe? Was I too stressed, did I not sleep enough, did I sleep on my back too late into the pregnancy, did I exercise too hard, or did I not exercise hard enough? Maybe I took the wrong vitamins, or not enough vitamins.

It turns out he had what the doctors called microtia, or in layman's terms, "small ear." Through a series of tests, we discovered that he also had a heart condition called pulmonic stenosis.

After a couple surgeries, a lot of doctor's visits, and a tremendous amount of worry and blaming myself, I've learned to appreciate Owen more. Every piece of his life and this experience dealing with his health challenges has been a true miracle and a blessing.

When you go through something difficult, it causes you to wake up a little. I had to learn to stop blaming myself, and that made me appreciate so much about this little guy. What a little fighter. Most days I forget all about his birth defects. He's just a happy little guy, living his life without a care in the world but teaching me so much.

When I look back at all the stepping stones that led me to where I am now and the life I've created, I see that each breakthrough happened because of the story, or influence, of another person.

What do you think? Does our influence really matter?

HECK YES!

Your story is unique. Only you have lived exactly what you've lived, and that creates a story that was meant to be shared. Your story is something that has impacted you in such a way that there's no turning back, and you are a completely changed person because of your experience. Your story can move others to take action in their own lives. You pave the way for them as you courageously share your life with others.

YOU may be the answer to someone else's prayer. So don't be afraid to put yourself out there. Talk to the girl sitting next to you at work, school, or church. Write that blog post, be the encourager, the example, the trail blazer.

The world needs YOU.

We are all influencers. What kind of an influencer do you want to be?

Chapter 3

Homeschool Dropout

If only I had a memory like an elephant, maybe I'd still remember how to do third-grade math.

As I mentioned in the last chapter, I did homeschool my kids for a few years. I wanted to be the perfect mom who does everything at amplified intensity, and at the time homeschooling felt like the perfect way to do this.

I'd like to take you back a few years to my homeschooling days. At the time, I only had three kids. Lily was six, Oliver was three, and Brooklyn was about ten months old. I wrote this on my blog one day in order to give everyone a little inside look at how my high expectations of being the perfect mom were doomed to fail:

Fall 2012

It's our first day of school. I'm anxious to begin and try out all the fun new ideas I found on Pinterest. I gather all the kids into the school room. I settle Brooklyn on the floor with a basket of toys, then begin reading a short devotional that was meant for the preschool mind. I barely read two words when Lily begins calling over to Brooklyn, trying to get her to smile. Oliver says to me, "Mom, this is boring." . . . *WHAT? I haven't even begun!* So

I rush through the devotional as Oliver heads for the door. *He has to go potty.* Lily says she's hungry, *even though we just had breakfast.* I tell her we'll have lunch after we're done with school. She insists that she's starving. I try to convince her that school won't take long and we'll have a break for lunch soon, at the same time I'm feeling slightly guilty, thinking that perhaps she IS hungry and therefore can't focus on the lesson. I compromise by telling her to just do one handwriting worksheet, and then we'll take a break.

Oliver is yelling from the bathroom for me to wipe his bum. Brooklyn's starting to get fussy and Lily is complaining that her worksheet is too hard. I rush to Oliver to wipe his bum only to find poop all over the toilet seat and somehow on his foot. *Don't know how that's possible.* By the time I get Oliver all cleaned up, Brooklyn is now screaming. She's hungry and ready for her nap. I take her upstairs while telling the kids to be quiet so I can put Brooklyn down for a nap. As I'm nursing Brooklyn to sleep, I hear Oliver screaming at the top of his lungs. I hurry to put Brooklyn in her crib, but she's startled by Oliver's screaming. She begins to cry, but I leave her anyway. Close her bedroom door and rush down to see what's the matter. Apparently Lily has decided she wants the stuffed animal Oliver was playing with. It belongs to Lily, but the minute she saw Olly playing with it, she decides NOW she wants it. I tell her to give it to Olly. She insists that it's her very special one and nobody can play with it. By now my anxiety levels are through the roof. I try to remain calm and tell them they need to share. All three kids are now crying . . . My patience is gone, and I yell . . . *Yes, I yell sometimes.*

They stop fighting. Brooklyn finally falls asleep. I take a deep breath and try once again to gather the kids back into the school room, this time with snacks. I plop down on the couch, lacking the enthusiasm I started with. I already feel like I need a break. *Maybe I'll go get on the treadmill real quick*, I think to myself. Putting my headphones on and getting lost in my workout sounds really nice right about now. I know that if I don't take advantage of Brooklyn's nap time, I may not get my workout in at all today. So I tell the kids we'll finish school as soon as I'm done on the treadmill. I put on an educational video and tell them they need to watch it. They begin to protest and say those movies are boring and they want to watch something else. I tell them that they can choose the movie for bedtime, but during the day they have to watch something that helps them learn. They continue to whine as I slide the DVD in and push play. I get on the treadmill.

Of course I'm interrupted about five minutes into it. They are asking if they can have a treat. "After lunch," I say. Oliver cries and lays down on the floor next to the treadmill. He continues to cry, and I turn up my music on my headphones, trying to drown out the crying. Finally he stops but decides he wants to play with his toys right next to me. I tell him not to play by the treadmill while it's on. He insists that he'll be careful. He disappears behind me, which then of course makes me panic. "Go play somewhere else," I say sternly. He leaves the room finally, but it's obvious his feelings were hurt. I feel bad, so I cut my workout short and run after him to give him loves. I decide I'd better get some lunch for them.

We have lunch, I clean up the house a little, and then I head back into the school room. This time I only have Lily. Oliver has left a trail of toys all over the house. He's happily playing with his dinosaurs, so I decide to let him be. I begin reading to Lily from our history book. As I'm reading to her, I'm feeling really good about our time together. Just as I think she's showing interest in the story, she says, "How many more pages, Mom?" Now I'm irritated again. I try not to show it, though, and say, "I'm almost done."

After the history lesson, I pull out her math workbook. As I lay it in front of her, she instantly complains that she HATES math and she doesn't want to do it. I tell her she can't play with friends later if she doesn't complete her schoolwork. "No, PLEASE can I have a friend over?" she whines. I once again say, "AFTER your school work is done." "Well, can I have a break first?" she says. *Ugh, are you serious? We've barely accomplished anything today, and it's already 3:00.*

Brooklyn wakes up from her nap, Oliver wants me to play dinosaurs with him, and Lily is sitting in the school room complaining she can't do her math. I bring Brooklyn into the school room and sit with Lily as I show her how to count her fingers for math. I know she's just not trying at all. We're doing simple addition and she's acting like it's all new to her. As I walk her through EVERY single problem, I'm holding Brooklyn on my lap, trying to bridle her eager fists from pulling out my hair.

We finally finish the math. By now I'm completely exhausted. I decide we're done for the day. I'm feeling stressed and upset about how the day went. I go over to Sean's office and impulsively I tell him, "I'm not doing homeschool anymore!" "Uh, can we talk about this later? I'm in the middle of work," says Sean in a slightly annoyed tone. I storm out of his office even more mad than I was before. I believe I even slammed the door. *Yes, I felt pretty immature.*

I begin to cry . . . I daydream for a minute about how much easier it would be if I just sent Lily back to public school. I say a prayer and ask for strength to endure. Later that night Sean comes in from working (his office is located in our backyard above our detached garage). By then I've calmed down a little. He knows I didn't mean what I said and just gives me a hug. I cry a little more.

After the kids go to bed, we have a long talk about our goals with homeschool and try to come up with some ways to motivate Lily. Sean helps me calm down, reassures me that we will be fine, and tells me to stop putting so much pressure on myself.

A few days pass, and things begin to get better. Lily is cooperating and showing a better attitude. Oliver is getting used to the fact that he needs to sit still and be quiet if he wants to be in the school room with us. We take advantage of Brooklyn's nap by doing as much school as we can. I've started inviting other homeschoolers over to do schoolwork with Lily, which has really motivated her. She is now ASKING to do math.

I've hired some help to come in and do the housework for me in order to maintain my sanity. And I have Lily play with Brooklyn while I get my workout in.

Now

The truth is, homeschooling was HARD! But most things worth doing aren't easy. I like to compare a lot of things to my volunteer service in Germany. That was the hardest eighteen months of my life, but it was also a time that rendered much growth. It formed me into a better person with finer work ethic and less focus on myself. It also helped me with the ability to get along with a roommate (i.e., a husband).

What I'm trying to convey here is *yes*, homeschooling wasn't what I thought it would be. I imagined blissful days of learning, going on nature walks, creating art, and lots of reading and snuggles in a perfectly clean home. It was far from that. This expectation caused me to feel frustrated a lot of the time. I blamed my kids for not cooperating, and I blamed Sean for not saying and doing the right things. There were all kinds of reasons I came up with in my head that explained why things weren't going the way I wanted.

I finally came to the conclusion that it was all me. Instead of focusing so much on everything being perfect, I just needed to be accepting, patient, loooooong suffering, and just love on my kids. That was the only way to maintain sanity in my role as a mother.

I believe we should never get too comfortable in life. We've got to find a balance between simplifying our lives and pushing ourselves a little too. We must be faced with challenges in order to be molded into the amazing people we are destined to become.

Fast forward to the present day. My kids are now in public school. They were really excited about this transition, and to be honest, so was I. They were excited about something new and the social aspect of public school, and they love the fact that they get to ride the bus. You know, the important things.

Let me tell you why I chose to homeschool in the first place. Basically, what happened was Lily started kindergarten. It was kind of a wake-up call for me. I was like, *Oh my, the time really is going fast.* People always tell you to cherish those times with your kids because it goes by so quickly. The fact that Lily would now be going to school every day really freaked me out. I was worried I didn't teach her enough or spend enough time with her. I worried about having regrets later in life.

I started having those thoughts during Lily's first month of kindergarten in public school. As a result, I started researching everything about homeschool. One night I met up with a bunch of homeschooling moms so I could ask them all my questions. After I left the meet-up, I decided right then and there that homeschooling was what I wanted.

Lily ended up getting sick with the flu the very next day, and I saw it as the perfect opportunity to pull her out of public school. I didn't tell her we were officially homeschooling, and she never even asked about her public-school class.

We went on field trips, read lots of books, and did crafts and art projects. Those are the things that I wanted to do together. I felt extremely proud of myself as a mother that first year of homeschooling. It was a great year, full of fun family time with no distractions from friends.

Then the second year came along. It was equally as beautiful, if not more so because I was preparing for a natural home birth with Brooklyn. It was so amazing that Lily got to be so much a part of that pregnancy. She went with me to all of my appointments and got to hear the baby's heartbeat and learn about the process of the baby growing inside me. Those times were moments that I will cherish forever. She got to be there when Brooklyn was born and then spend all day, every day with her newborn baby sister. I just loved it and felt so happy and content.

Toward the end of that school year is when I started to feel overwhelmed. Brooklyn wasn't sleeping so much during the day, and Oliver decided he was done with naps. The nap time was what had given Lily and I time to focus on schoolwork.

I ended up putting Lily in public school for the last month of her first-grade year, for me and for her, because I wanted to give her that experience. The end of the year is all fun and games, so I thought it would be fun for her to go on field trips and have "hat day" and "pajama day" and enjoy all the fun parties and games they do at the end of the school year.

Then the third year came, and I thought, *Okay . . . what am I going to do? I am really stressed.* Brooklyn was eighteen months old, and that's a busy time, *am I right?* I felt overwhelmed and worried that I couldn't survive another year. I knew that I was capable of handling it, and I knew many other moms did it with more kids and more babies, but I just didn't feel I was up for the challenge. So I put her in public school for that third year but still homeschooled her a few months within that year.

Then I got pregnant with Owen, and life continued to get busier. That's also when I quit blogging. Feeling overwhelmed was an understatement when pregnancy hormones were added on top of everything.

At the time, I totally believed in homeschooling and had a hard admitting I no longer wanted to do it. I pride myself in having leadership qualities, but to be completely honest, I'm not always a leader. My natural tendencies revolve around fitting in. I love being part of a community and being in social environments, so for me to be the only one in the neighborhood homeschooling was really tough on me. I wanted to fit in. I didn't like the feeling I was having among my friends. They didn't intentionally leave me out, but it just happened.

I always felt a little awkward talking about homeschool. I didn't ever want to come across as self-righteous or make others think that I thought I was better than them. I believe that we as mothers know what's best for our own children, and homeschooling is not always the best option.

I loved homeschooling, and I love public school. My mom didn't homeschool me when I was growing up, so I had great memories of being in elementary school. If anything, I would skip the junior high years all together.

Another thing I realized is that my kids are willing to do their work for their teachers but are not always so cooperative for me. I also didn't enjoy doing the schoolwork. I just wanted to do the fun stuff—the creative art projects and field trips—and feel free to learn whatever we wanted to learn. Time together was my motivation behind homeschooling. It wasn't because I felt I could give my kids a better education or because I wasn't impressed with the teachers, the classes, or the school system. It had nothing to do with that. I simply wanted to make sure I had that time with my kids while they were still young and still WANTED to be with me.

I have definitely gained a lot more respect for teachers through this experience. It is kind of nice to hand that responsibility over to the public school so I can focus on the fun stuff, like life lessons and spiritual growth. When it comes to math and grammar, that's just not fun for me.

As mothers, we just want to do everything right for our kids. But what I've learned is that there are no right or wrong choices. Whatever you choose to do is exactly the way it's supposed to be. Just enjoy the ride, and don't beat yourself up when things don't go the way you envision or you change your mind about a particular path you had chosen for your kids. Allow yourself to experiment, and pivot when needed.

Chapter 4

Discovering Your Mission and Purpose

Every year I put on an event for women. I call it the "Wannabe Balanced | Women Empowerment Event." It was born out of sheer desire to help others connect with their individual purposes and missions in life. I believe each of us has something so unique and different to offer. The hard parts are discovering what it is and having the courage to move forward into action. We get discouraged by oversaturated markets and our underdeveloped skills. The result is unintentionally withholding our gifts from the world.

It's funny how things happen in our lives that prepare us for the next "event." About a month before my 2018 Wannabe Balanced event, I had an unexpected experience. Because of my intense quest to discover more about our individual purposes, I attracted a newfound awareness into my life. I was given a broader perspective on the way I viewed life in general. I would even call it an awakening.

I had a breakthrough unlike anything I ever experienced in my life. But before I had the breakthrough, I had to have a breakdown (I share more about this in chapter six). The breakdown felt so intense that I couldn't imagine my life moving forward. I wanted to cancel the event, quit podcasting, and forget about writing this book all together. Thank goodness I didn't act impulsively amongst the suffering of my mental collapse. Eventually I came out of it and was given advanced perspective, which rendered overflowing inspiration for my event and for this book.

Moral of the story: be careful what you wish for.

Breakthroughs always start with a breakdown. That combination becomes your story. Your story inspires your mission, and your mission is what gives you purpose.

Our greatest desire in life is to be happy, and being happy comes from connecting to our higher self so that we can reach our full potential and be guided in the right direction to fulfill the special mission that was designed just for us. We crave knowing what we are made of, knowing why we are here, and understanding what our purpose is and how it is unique only to us. We want to know and understand what makes us special.

Usually our purpose or message is something that we have a deep connection with. It's filled with experience and surrounded with emotion that has us so evolved that we can't help but share what we have learned. We all have the desire to share happiness. Once you've tasted the fruit of peace and joy, you want everyone to have a slice of the pie, especially the ones you love most.

Everyone has a story to share. Everyone has a special mission, and everyone has a unique set of gifts that were meant to be discovered and used in this life. Unexpressed ideas and contributions don't just go away; they are likely to eat away at your soul until eventually they make their way out in the form of resentment, depression, anxiety, boredom, overeating, anger, or rage.

> There is a vitality, a life force, an energy, a quickening that is translated through you into action, and because there is only one of you in all of time, this expression is unique. And if you block it, it will never exist through any other medium and it will be lost. The world will not have it. It is not your business to determine how good it is nor how valuable nor how it compares with other expressions. It is your business to keep it yours clearly and directly, to keep the channel open. You do not even have to believe in yourself or your work. You have to keep yourself open and aware to the urges that motivate you. Keep the channel open.[1]

When I think of all the challenging things I've done in my life, like putting on a big event, homeschooling my kids, running a marathon, writing a book, giving birth naturally, and serving an eighteen-month Christian mission, I find myself at one point or another wondering why I *chose* to do those things in the first place. Why did I put this unnecessary weight on my shoulders?

Why?

Because the weight makes us stronger, and as spiritual beings having a human experience, we crave growth. It's not enough for us to sit idle in our lives. We may *think* that's what we want, a life of ease and pleasure. But ultimately, it's more painful when we don't do hard things. The easier road is much less fulfilling. It's the hard things that not only enlighten us of our true potential and empower us to achieve more but also uncover little by little who we are, how we are unique, and what we can ultimately become.

> There's nothing wrong with living a safe life, except that NOT pursuing your dreams is more painful than working through the fear and overwhelm that comes with going for it.[2]

Like Les Brown says in his motivational speeches, "Do what is easy and your life will be hard; do what is hard and your life will be easy."

What Drives You?

In the past, I struggled with understanding my motivation behind the things I did, like blogging, creating YouTube videos, podcasting, or writing a book. I questioned my own intentions based on the opinions of others and then felt ashamed at the thought that perhaps I had a need for attention or approval—like I had deep-seated issues and was trying to fill some sort of void with others' approval.

I learned that contribution is a basic human need. I'm embarrassed to admit that I didn't know this desire to contribute is inherent in all of us. You know the scripture that says, "The truth shall make you free" (see John 8:32)? This *truth* literally set me *free* from my own judgments that I put on myself. I realized that my motivations are healthy, pure, and completely normal. We are children of God, the creator of the universe, which means we too were designed to create and contribute to his beautiful masterpiece.

> God left the world unfinished for man to work his skill upon. He left the electricity in the cloud, the oil in the earth. He left the rivers unabridged and the forests unfelled and the cities unbuilt. God gives to man the challenge of raw materials, not the ease of finished things. He leaves the pictures unpainted and the music unsung and the problems unsolved, that man might know the joys and glories of creation.[3]

Sometimes we get so caught up in achieving the BIG goals that we forget what is most important. The one thing that only *you* can do is be a mother to your children, a wife to your husband, or a daughter to your parents. So when it comes to figuring out your purpose and your mission in life, it MUST start with the ones you love most, and then it can trickle out into the rest of world.

This is not to say that we shouldn't pursue anything other than being a wife and mother. This is one thing that has had me confused more often than not. I've spent many hours pondering this and feeling guilty over doing things that didn't particularly have to do with my role as a mother. When you take the time for personal development and growth, you enhance your mothering abilities. You become more equipped to teach your children the tools for navigating adult life and becoming who God designed them to be. Not only do you become a better teacher, but the example that you're setting for them is crucial for their growth. What kind of an example do you want to be? Do you want to be a mother who knows her value and therefore takes time to herself, caters to her needs for growth, prayer, learning, meditation, and developing her talents?

Often times, I hear women say they just don't know what they're passionate about or whether or not they even have any gifts or talents. It's a common concern, but my advice is to just start trying things. Life is about experimenting, and in the process of experimentation, you will discover your passion.

When I was twenty-one, I wrote out a "life list." It was a list of all the things I wanted to do or try out in my life. Little by little, I've worked down the list, and it has become a process of elimination. I try something out and decide if it's something I really like and could become passionate about. Some things only last a month, and some last a few years.

But What If It Was All a Waste of Time?

There is no such thing as a waste of time because everything we choose to spend our time on teaches us valuable life lessons and becomes a stepping stone toward self-discovery. As I look back at all the things I've tried but failed at, I can see how the pieces connect to create the beautiful masterpiece in the end.

We discover what we like by doing, not thinking. At times I've found myself completely paralyzed in my attempts to write a blog post or create a YouTube video. I started allowing myself to create less-than-perfect work in an attempt to just DO and not wait around trying to decide *what* to do, how to do it, if it is good enough, and what people would think. I just put one foot in front of the other and began taking action even when I didn't know exactly how I was going to do it.

I have a goal to create a new YouTube video each week. On Tuesday, I have a babysitter come while I spend time creating my video, preparing for my podcast episode, and writing my blog post. This past week, on Monday, I was feeling completely uninspired. I had no clue what kind of video to create. I tried finding reasons why I could just skip that week. Excuses like *It's not like anyone will really notice if I skip a week*, *I don't have to do this*, *I've had a cold*, *It's been a busy week*, and so on.

It is my goal to help others by sharing bits and pieces of my life and what I'm learning, but I also do it for myself in a way. It's about being the kind of person I want to be, by honoring my own commitments to myself. I want to be a person that continues to create and, most importantly, does what she says she's going to do. I call it the three Cs: **C**onsistently **C**reate with **C**onfidence.

So instead of throwing in the towel and deciding to quit, I searched Google for ideas, picked the first one on the list, and went for it with no expectations of it even being a great video. Instead, I did it simply for the sake of being consistent.

As I started filming the video footage, ideas just started coming to me, and it turned out to be one of my favorite videos. I'm not sure if others thought that the same, but I'm getting a lot better at appreciating my own work even if others don't. I've realized that whenever I put too much expectation around the outcome of how it's perceived by others on social media, I quickly lose enthusiasm for what I do. And when I really take time to analyze what happened, I realize that I genuinely enjoy the process of creating, but it's putting expectations on the outcome that ruins it for me.

What Keeps Us from Creating and Contributing?

Thoughts like

- *People might think I'm a bad mom for spending time on this.*
- *People might think I want attention.*
- *What if it's stupid and no good?*
- *I don't know HOW I can contribute.*
- *It's already been done before.*
- *I don't want others to be intimidated or feel jealousy toward me.*

One day I was chatting with one of my friends. She was telling me about her twin daughters, who were extremely talented at dancing. They had spent most of their lives in competitive dance and were now seniors in high school. They were both on the drill team.

She was explaining to me how her daughters have had a really hard time because of their beauty and talent. Other girls were mean to them. So, being a concerned mother, she told her girls to minimize their talent. *Don't do your best, and always stay on the back row as to not draw any attention to yourselves*, she advised.

As mothers, we want nothing more for our children than to be loved and accepted, especially during one of the hardest seasons of life, *the dreaded teenage years*.

Although I can totally relate to this mother's intentions and don't know exactly what I would do in this situation, I do believe that playing small so others will feel good about themselves is no way to live your life.

> We ask ourselves
> Who am I to be brilliant, gorgeous, talented, fabulous?
> Actually, who are you *not* to be?
> Your playing small
> does not serve the world.
> There is nothing enlightened about shrinking so that other people won't feel insecure around you.[4]

I remember when I first began my blog I was talking with one of my friends about it and shared how I was really excited about blogging. She responded with, "Yeah, well, there are just so many bloggers already."

As you can imagine, this killed my enthusiasm a bit and I felt a tad discouraged. After all, she was right. Did we really need more bloggers in the world?

YES! We do need more bloggers. We need more of whatever it is you feel called to do. There is more than enough room, and there is an endless supply of opportunity in this world. The scarcity mentality is what keeps us from pursuing things that have already been done before. When we look around and see so many doing what we want to do, and doing it well, we tend to believe there's no room for us. But the more we adapt an abundance mentality, the less competitive and the happier we will become.

Contribute to Spreading Positive Messages

When we think of how everything has already been done before, why not think the thought, *I'm going to contribute to spreading that positive message?*

What we fail to realize is that successful contribution doesn't always show up in numbers on social media. So many of us, including myself, get so caught up in the outward appearance of success that we don't realize all we have accomplished that was simply not posted on social media.

Social media is such a wonderful tool for women in business and even women all over the world looking for like-minded, supportive friends. But it can also be used against us if we don't learn the tools that keep us out of the comparison and envy trap. *See chapter fifteen for more on this topic.*

Why We Quit

Whenever I've pursued different things over the years, there would always come a point when it got really hard or didn't seem to be working out the way I wanted it to. In the past, I used to take this to mean it wasn't "meant to be" and probably was not what God wanted me to do. Over time, I realized that the hardest point is usually right when we're about to reach the top. Sadly, too many of us quit at the most crucial time. If you keep going just a little further, you'll find yourself at the top. When you get there, you'll see your effort was worth the pain. You'll finally get the chance to rest for a bit and appreciate all the beauty around you.

Pursuing your dreams is not always fun. Sometimes we look at others who are really going after their dreams and have achieved tremendous success. We think, *Life must be so good for them. Look at them living their dreams.* But if you take the time to learn about their journey getting there, you'll realize that although some find their passion, create massive influence, become an expert, or make millions doing what they love, it doesn't mean it was all unicorns and rainbows. Neither do you eventually get to a point in your life when everything becomes easy and blissful all the time.

We tend to think that once we reach our goals we will feel a certain way—happy, content, at peace, etc. Yes, those feelings come with every great achievement, but life wasn't meant to be amazing ALL the time. We cannot taste the sweet without the bitter, and this applies to our entire lives. We will always have good days and bad days, no matter the success we have achieved.

As we are ever-evolving beings, we will always be striving for more. The goal is to be striving for more and at the same time being filled with so much gratitude for what we have, our abilities, the life we've created thus far, and the abundance of blessings that God continues to offer us as we do our part by taking action.

Notes

1. Martha Graham, as quoted by Agnes De Mille in *Martha: The Life and Work of Martha Graham*, 264.
2. Jody Moore, Boldnewmom.com.
3. Thomas S. Monson, "In Quest of the Abundant Life," *Ensign*, Mar. 1988.
4. Marianne Williamson, *A Return to Love*. (New York: HarperCollins, 1992), 191.

Chapter 5

But I Don't Want to Change

Change is an inevitable part of life, and it's also a part that we dread the most. We want to remain comfortable at the same time we crave growth. So we muddle through the parts of change that we don't like in order to get to the other side, where we feel a taste of euphoria.

There is no better feeling than self-mastery, overcoming, and achieving. But there are parts of the change process that drive us insane and can cause us to give up on our dreams. Changing our lives, our habits, and our thoughts can become so intense at times that we wonder if it's even possible for us to get the result we want. Then we begin making excuses and justifications that eventually talk us out of trying in the first place.

I believe change and striving for the seemingly impossible can be a much smoother undertaking if you understand the steps and process a little more clearly.

You may recall from previous chapters that when I was pregnant with Brooklyn, I suddenly became interested in natural birth. I never in a million years thought I'd be one to give birth naturally. I've always been kind of a wimp when it comes to pain, and I wasn't afraid of drugs in the least. So I was just as shocked as everyone else when I made the decision to go unmedicated. I was freaking out internally, thinking, *What the heck am I getting myself into?* But when I commit to something, I'm pretty determined to follow through. I wrote a full blog post about my decision and hesitated a little before clicking "publish." I knew that once I made it public, that was it. I would have to follow through—otherwise I'd look like an idiot.

I'm glad I wrote the blog post and put it out there, but it also opened the floodgates of negative and startling feedback. Everyone suddenly wanted to share their horror stories and intimidate me away from having a baby at home and not in the hospital. This was really hard and filled my mind with excessive fear—fear of the unknown.

Thankfully, I was able to get past some of the panic and focus on my goal. I found myself a midwife and tried researching as much as possible to prepare myself for what I understood to be the most bitter pain *ever.*

Some people might wonder why any woman would choose to put herself through such unnecessary torture when we have modern medicine that allows us to forfeit that misery. I agree that we are so fortunate to have the amazing doctors and scientists today that have worked extensively to save us women from the agony of childbirth. I mean, seriously, what was God thinking when He came up with the plan of procreation? Why is the contribution that men provide all based on pleasure while women were assigned the suffering? Doesn't seem fair, now does it?

Well, I guess the other way of looking at it is God designed us this way for a reason. We are powerful beyond measure, and any time we endure something so extreme, it transforms us into the next best version of ourselves. Childbirth and many other life-altering events require us to walk through the depths of despair. Martha Beck compares this to a caterpillar in a cocoon. The caterpillar doesn't just grow wings and become a butterfly;

it literally melts down into a liquid, and then it begins to form into an entirely different creature.[1]

This is also the case in life. When we have the desire to change and become a beautiful butterfly, it requires intensity to the point of a meltdown. Childbirth is a gift from God, one of His beautiful ways to empower us women, who throughout history have been suppressed and treated as weaker than men. More and more, our society is recognizing the breathtaking power and strength that women possess.

Back to my first home-birth story. When I went into labor, I remember feeling so excited and highly prepared. I thought I knew exactly what to expect and how to have a relaxing labor and easy delivery.

When I realized I was officially in labor, I immediately called everyone over: Melissa Mayo (my midwife), my doula, and my photographer. My labor was progressing very quickly, and I was already at seven centimeters by the time Melissa arrived. I thought, *Really? I'm already seven centimeters? This hasn't been too painful. Maybe I'm just one of those lucky women that have easy labors and painless childbirths.*

Boy, was I wrong. Once everyone came over, the labor slowed down for a while. It was the calm before the storm. Suddenly things became more intense than I could even imagine. I thought, *GET ME OUT OF THIS! WHY DID I CHOOSE THIS? WHAT WAS I THINKING? THIS IS TOO INTENSE. I CAN'T DO THIS!*

It all seemed to last forever, almost to the point where I literally thought I was going to die. I pushed and pushed through the most intense contractions, and after I endured hours of excruciating pain, her head emerged slightly. It only came out halfway as I was screaming for someone to just pull her out. I kept asking, *Why can't you just pull her out now? Please just pull her out!*

"We can't help you here. YOU must push harder. You are the only one that can do this!" exclaimed Melissa.

So a few more contractions later *plus the loudest screaming I've ever voiced*, baby Brooklyn arrived. We all gently pulled her to the surface of the water and placed her on my chest. At that moment I was overwhelmed with emotions. I was relieved, empowered, and a completely changed woman. It was the absolute hardest thing I had ever experienced, but somehow at the same time, it was the most incredible miracle I had ever witnessed. I was completely blown away by the God-given strength and endurance He put in women to perform such a miracle.

At the same time, I remember saying, "I'm NEVER doing that again."

And just three years later, I found myself doing it all over again. The reward you get from doing something so unbelievably hard, and the change that happens within as you strive to do hard things, keeps you coming back for more.

The second time was a much smoother experience. The pain was just as intense, but I went into the labor with a new set of skills and understanding. I knew exactly what to expect, and I went into it with a different strategy. During my pregnancy, I spent a lot more time preparing myself mentally, reading books and listening to hypno birthing audios with positive affirmations and subliminal messages.

When the labor started, I was very calm. I texted Melissa but didn't tell her to come over just yet. I wanted to labor on my own as long as possible because I had learned a few things from Brooklyn's birth. Inviting everyone over too soon actually caused me to tense up, which resulted in slowing down the labor. I felt pressure to perform. Thoughts like *It's late, I feel bad they are missing out on sleep for me*, and *I need to hurry and have this baby so they can all get home and go to bed* interfered with the experience.

My labor started at midnight. At 3:00 a.m. I called everyone over, and at 4:00 a.m. baby Owen was born. It was beautiful and amazing, but again I told myself, *I'm NEVER doing this again.*

I realized, though, that experience, mixed with knowledge and tools, provided a much smoother birth. Like I said, the delivery was just as painful, but the labor was shorter.

In summary, knowing what to expect from the experience, being equipped with additional knowledge about the process of labor and delivery, and creating new strategies helped me tremendously the second time around.

In a similar fashion, when we know the different phases of change, then we understand what to expect and are less likely to jump ship when things get tough. We understand that no emotion lasts forever. There must be opposition in all things, which means that when things are really tough, they are bound to get really good. It's the law of the universe and has proven to be true since the beginning of time.

Despite our resistance to change, it is bound to happen. It happens slowly from within, it's brought on by life's inevitable circumstances, or it comes along due to opportunities presented.

In her book *Finding Your Own North Star*, Martha Beck teaches the four phases of change.

The first phase she describes as the death of an old life and the birth of a new one. This is your moment when you get to choose a new you and organize a new life course.

When I got married, I lost my best friend from high school. I didn't lose her to some tragic accident, although it felt like death to me. It was the death of my adolescent life and the birth of a new one as a married woman. I tried so hard to remain the same person I was in high school in an attempt to hold on to that friendship, but it proved to be disastrous. It just isn't possible to be the crazy flirty, fly-by-the-seat-of-your-pants kind of gal when you're a newlywed trying to be unified in a new life together. I still feel tremendous love for my teenage BFF, but I had to accept the fact that some relationships have a lifespan, and that is not a bad thing. We created so many wonderful memories together, she was there for me when my family wasn't, and she had my back through every breakup and stupid decision I made as a teenager.

The second phase is when you suddenly begin dreaming and visualizing your new life. You start creating the blueprint.

Phase three is the time to put your dreams into action. As you begin taking action, you discover it's not easy. You try and fail, and fail to try. Often times this is the phase where people give up. They take their failures as a sign that it isn't meant to be or maybe they are just no good at it. But instead of throwing in the towel, you must keep going. You just need to learn to make necessary modifications, and eventually you'll discover what works for you.

Phase four is the time to relax and enjoy the fruits of your labors . . . Until the next catalytic event happens.[2]

My husband, Sean, has a really inspiring success story that I wanted him to share:

Sean

When I started in my own small business, I had very little experience in such endeavors. I was in my early twenties, and I was overflowing with ambition. I personified "ignorance on fire!" My goal was simple: to never have to work for another human being ever in my entire life. I wanted to be a millionaire by the time I was thirty and retire by forty. Sounds good, right? I was a dreamer—you can't knock that. I was naïve, though. My lack of experience set me up for some rough lessons and a harsh reality. I just assumed that a person could open up the doors to their business, and then good things would start to happen. This is why many of us businessmen believe that starting your own business might be as beneficial as a college education, even if you fail! We certainly do learn more from our failures than from our successes.

That first year I was really actively researching, creating, promoting, branding, selling products, and following up with customers—you know, all the things you are supposed to do in business. I achieved some success, although limited, in my view, and it certainly didn't stack up anywhere with what I saw other people in my industry doing. I remember at one point after that first year, I sat and took inventory of my business and my results. It was a sobering experience. I realized that I would have earned more by working for minimum wage at a local fast food restaurant than what I had earned in my own personal business venture! This experience was incredibly disheartening, and I became unmotivated. I found myself in a funk for probably six months' time, and then I snapped out of it with the help of wonderful mentors and training that I came across. Some of this training was centered around a couple of analogies that have really stuck with me even fifteen years later. I love analogies and stories that cause us to think deeply on our own. This is my preferred method of learning. I'll share these powerful analogies with you now.

First of all, I was made aware of a phenomenon that we have all personally witnessed but probably failed to acknowledge or comprehend. To set the stage, I want you to think about something that you witnessed getting built, like a new house, a store, a commercial office space, or a hotel. You might even be aware of something getting built right now. There is something amazing about these buildings. The majority of the time required to build them is spent below ground, on stuff you cannot see! You may be exposed to a new building project for many months and think to yourself, *My goodness, it is taking them* forever *to get that thing going, let alone built!*

You see, what we do not understand is that there is so much that goes into the building process that we cannot see, below ground. You have to do all of the site planning, zoning, architecture, engineering, excavating, dealing with water drainage. You have to bring all of the utilities, digging large trenches and tying into existing services or bringing them from wherever they currently are. Then there are the forms for the footings and foundation, everything that is going to keep that building standing in the event of something like an earthquake. Oh, and I failed to mention the process of working with the city, all of the permitting and inspections. They literally inspect every single thing you do and consider the safety, longevity, and impact that this building might have on neighboring structures and the environment. Personally, I am not a contractor or builder of such structures, so I am probably leaving a lot of things out—in fact, I *know* I am leaving out a lot. Bottom line, everything that must be accomplished below ground can take many months! The phenomenon I previously referred to occurs once the builders are able to get above ground and start throwing up walls. Once they make it above ground, things progress at what seems like light speed! I have personally come upon a completed home in my neighborhood and remarked to Crystal, "Where the heck did that home come from?" The same goes for a hotel; once they get above ground, they are able to dramatically accelerate their progress as you witness floor after floor going up relatively quickly. It feels like you could practically sit there and watch the building go up in real time in a matter of days.

Another analogy that really hit home for me was the concept of an old water pump, like what you would find on an old farm. These pumps have handles attached to them so that you can pump the water up from its source. The trick to these old pumps is that the water does not flow immediately. You have to prime the pump with extensive pumping to build pressure like a vacuum in order to get that water to effectively defy gravity and make its way up to you. If you didn't know any better, you might pump the handle ten times or so and then stop, assuming that it was broken. In order to get that initial flow, you must pump persistently for what might feel like several minutes. In reality, it probably only takes about thirty seconds, but if you are pumping fast, it does feel like an awful lot of work. Even when the water does arrive, it does not do so in great abundance. It will start as a small stream, and as before, steady, consistent pumping is required to gradually build a steady flow with substantive volume. Certainly not what we are used to in the modern age, where we simply turn a knob and have instant water at our disposal!

These analogies apply to almost any endeavor that we might embark upon. Should we have an unreasonable expectation, like I did for my business early on, we will ultimately find ourselves frustrated and defeated. If we only had the proper perspective, we would know that anything worthwhile takes time to build. Like a beautiful building, anything that is going to stand the test of time and the elements will take time to build.

It is an investment of sorts. The investment of time below ground as we build a structure yields a return of accelerated growth once above ground. The time needed to achieve such results can vary depending on the landscape, the environment, and the experience of the builder. The same can be said about the water pump. The investment of time, pumping away repeatedly in a rapid manner, will yield a return in the form of a steady flow of water.

There are things that I like in particular about both analogies. I like that in the building example, you only have to build it once. If done right, it will yield a benefit for many years to come, most likely hundreds of years. I would like to mention that even once the building is complete, routine care, maintenance, and updating are critical to ensure longevity.

Think deeply about all of the parallels you can find here for your business. I know people who built their businesses fast and got their income up, but because they did not build a solid, sturdy foundation, their success is not self-sustaining. I know people who thought that once the water arrived, it would naturally just keep coming on its own forever without a care. They pay a big price when that water dries up and they have to start all over, seemingly from scratch, to get that business going again.

Should you remain patient and steadfast in your good business practices, committed to the ultimate vision and mission, you will eventually realize sustained success. When you do, I highly encourage you to never take your finger off the pulse of your business or organization, even though you may not ever have to work so hard again as you did in the beginning. Let's hope you did it right so that you won't.[3]

Notes

1. Martha Beck, "Growing Wings: The Power of Change," https://marthabeck.com/2003/01/growing-wings-the-power-of-change.
2. Martha Beck, *Finding Your Own North Star* (New York: Random House, 2001), chapters 11–15.
3. Also at http://escobargroup.blogspot.com/2018/07/2-great-analogies-for-any-business.html; used with permission.

Chapter 6

The Breakdown before the Breakthrough

In the process of writing this book, I've been searching deep into all the experiences of my life that have been turning points in my personal development. Until recently, I always felt like I had a hard time relating to depression and anxiety. I've definitely felt those emotions, but they have never lasted longer than a day. Even back in high school when I broke up with my boyfriend, I was definitely sad and it took me a while to get over him, but the intensity wasn't enough to send me into a deep, dark depression, as I know many have endured.

A few months ago, I experienced extreme fear, and it lasted for three days. I feared that maybe there was no purpose to life on earth and that everything was just random. This thought made me feel like I was literally going to die. It didn't feel natural that my body could actually undergo such potency of emotion. It was altogether unbearable. I know three days doesn't seem long when you compare it to someone who has been battling depression or anxiety for his or her entire life, but when you're experiencing such bitter emotion and it stays for days, you begin to wonder if it will ever go away. You begin fearing the fear itself, which just reinforces the power of it. At that point it becomes extremely difficult to regain control of your mind.

We all know that we create our own realities and what we think and believe is truly the baseline of what is actually real. So even though I knew this, it was hard to find thoughts that I could believe. Saying what you want to think in order to feel better doesn't necessarily work unless you can believe it. Faith is difficult to obtain when you're in complete darkness. But I now understand that experiencing the darkness is often what it takes in order to discover the light from within. As I've said before, my breakthrough was the result of a breakdown.

I had a full-on panic attack. I experienced this on an airplane once, but at least the flight was only an hour long, and I could get off and know I was safe. This recent panic attack felt the exact same, except it didn't go away after an hour or even a day. I felt that tightness in my stomach, the jitters in my body, I was sweating, crying, and pacing, and I felt nauseated, lightheaded, and like I was literally going insane. I tried to eat, hoping it would settle my stomach, but all I could manage to swallow were a few bites of bread or a cracker here and there. My mouth was so dry that I could barely get it down. I really felt like I couldn't go on—not that I was thinking suicidal thoughts or anything, but I literally thought this feeling was going to take me down completely.

Thank goodness for my husband. He took over the household while I was going through this. He held everything together while I was falling apart. I know he was incredibly worried for me and felt helpless at the time. Nothing anyone said or did could have helped me out of this. It had to happen from within.

When I trace back what happened that sent me into a downward spiral, I know exactly what it was. It wasn't just one thing but rather a series of events.

I had been reading many books lately, trying to gain all the knowledge I could to provide inspiration as I write this book and to create weekly podcast episodes. Little by little, I was becoming more open in my beliefs. I began to see things in a new light. It was fascinating and exciting all at the same time.

Until one moment I asked myself, "What if God doesn't even exist? What if everything we've believed has all been made up?"

This is something I'd never questioned before in my entire life because of the religious influence I was exposed to. I've just believed because everyone else believed. But when I thought this thought and imagined my life without God, it was just too much for my brain to handle. It's as though I asked this question and then instantly latched on to the belief that God didn't exist. I felt unbelievably small, alone, and overwhelmed with darkness, wondering why I was here and whether I really have a purpose. I felt like I was literally falling down a black hole and desperately trying to find something to grab on to, but there was nothing. At least for a while.

The turning point came when I finally started to relax into the fear. It felt like I was falling, but I was able to relax and enjoy it at the same time—as if I were skydiving, knowing that I had a parachute attached to me and I would safely land when the time was right. As I allowed the discomfort of fear to flow through me and as I quit resisting it, that's when I was able to take control of my mind once again. I found my core belief in God. Not the God that everyone taught me to believe in, but my own version of God. It was incredibly empowering to discover this from within and not based on anything I was taught growing up.

"Fear is excitement without breath."[1] I heard this in one of the books I've listened to recently called *The Big Leap*. I thought it was absolutely brilliant and made so much sense to me. Just as a roller coaster is exhilarating, so can be the feeling of fear. When we hold our breath, we transition into fear. So when we find ourselves overwhelmed with fear, we simply need to BREATHE, and we drop back down to a feeling of excitement. I'd much rather feel excitement.

I've been practicing this technique each time I begin to feel even the slightest bit of fear. I clear my mind and breathe until I get to a place of excitement. Once I'm in this place, I'm able to regain control over my thoughts and work on finding the true and believable ones at the same time I'm weeding out the made-up stories my brain offers me when I feel intense fear.

Just last week, I was at an amusement park and anxious to try out this whole "breathing through fear" thing. As I was riding one of the rides, I decided to take a deep breath in and then blow out at the point of highest intensity. You know when you're feeling the butterflies in your stomach? It's an automatic response to hold your breath. So instead of holding my breath, I took a nice deep breath in and out, and surprisingly, there were NO butterflies in my stomach. That sensation was completely nonexistent. I taught my kids this trick too, and they were shocked at the difference it made. We were excited to discover that this can work even when you're not REALLY scared, but your body just thinks it's scared.

Back to my breakdown. One thing I know for sure is that things always get better. Everything is constantly changing. We are evolving beings, which means that nothing ever stays the same—not negative emotions, and not even our knowledge and beliefs as a species. Since the beginning of time, we continue to discover new things. It's so exciting when you think about it, but I guess for me it was pretty dang scary. It's scary to be open to the "not knowing" of things. I love how Wayne Dyer advises us to be "open to everything and attached to nothing."[2] Sometimes we want to make everything so definitive and believe that any one person or religion has all the answers. It's like our brains just want something firm to hold on to. We want to believe we can predict the future and know exactly what is going to happen.

I'm finding peace in the not knowing because that means there's always more to discover. It's never the end; we never actually arrive. If we already knew everything there is to know about life, then what would motivate us to keep learning and trying new things? What would motivate us to connect with our inner guidance system to comfort and direct us?

It's funny how fear occurs; oftentimes it's not about what's happening in the moment—it's usually about the future, the "what ifs." In the moment, nothing bad was actually happening, and yet I was feeling as though I had literally lost a child. My kids were all happily playing and safe in our home. My husband was there. I had my health, my friends, and the wonderful life I had created. Everything in reality was beautiful and perfect, but I couldn't see it because I was thinking so far ahead into the future that I couldn't even acknowledge the beauty in the present moment.

Fear is my least favorite emotion, but it has its upside because it draws upon courage. And courage is something we can always use more of. Just as lifting weights strengthens your muscles, fear increases your volume of courage. So if you can go into feeling the fear with the knowledge of its strengthening power and what you're gaining in terms of personal growth, you'll feel a little more relaxed and able to allow it rather than defy it.

As I've been on this journey of spiritual growth and personal development, my biggest goal has been to simply be open to anything that feels like truth to me and focus on developing my personal connection with God.

I have to admit that making the decision to follow my own spiritual path was scary—hence the panic attack. I wanted to start from scratch, which meant throwing out everything I'd been taught to believe my whole life. I felt like the only way for me to discover personal truth was to start with nothing. I feared this path more than anything I've ever feared in my life, but I couldn't deny that it was my destiny. Little by little I'm gathering pieces from all religions, collecting what resonates with me, and leaving behind the things that don't.

The thing I feared most was how my relationship with God would be after I decided to follow my own path. Would I ever feel that peaceful feeling I'd felt in the past whenever I'd gone to God? Would that still be available, or did I just make it all up in my head? Did I really feel God before, or was it a lie I was telling myself because I wanted to fit in?

What I've discovered on this path is a deep connection unlike anything I have ever experienced. One night as I was meditating and pondering this, I felt an overwhelming feeling of love and peace that brought me to tears. I immediately told Sean what I had experienced and how I was so afraid that taking this path would mean never feeling that feeling again. I was overjoyed and full of gratitude knowing that God was there, He's always been there, and He will continue to be there for me the rest of my life no matter what path I choose. I no longer fear God or His judgments of my choices. I simply feel love.

In her book *The Universe Has Your Back*, Gabby Bernstein teaches ways of communicating with God or your inner being. One of her suggestions is to choose something that becomes your sign from God.[3] An animal, a number, a color, whatever you want. She chose the owl. So now any time she's searching for answers or signs from God, she looks for owls as manifestations of truth. This inspired me to do the same. My sign is the elephant. I chose this animal for many reasons. It all started when my book cover designer came to me with the idea of a mom and baby elephant as the symbol for the book. At first, I didn't see how elephants applied to my life as a "wannabe balanced mom." But the more I thought of it, the more I realized how divinely inspired this was, because elephants have in fact shown up multiple times in my life, one being when I first met Sean. We had only been on one date, and he had to leave town to attend the wedding of John Andersen, founder and creator of Isagenix. This wedding was the most elaborate wedding he had ever participated in. John sat upon an elephant as Sean led them into the ceremony, and John's bride, Cher, flew in on a helicopter. John, being the generous person he is, gave out crystals in the shape of elephants as gifts to all attending the wedding.

When Sean got home, he presented me with one of these crystal elephants. Now that gift has an even greater meaning to me. I've held onto that crystal elephant all these years, and I recently pulled it out of storage to place it in my new meditation station.

I've always been fascinated with elephants, and I've discovered many wonderful ways we can relate to these gentle giants. Of all animals, elephants are the most intelligent and most like humans in the sense that they experience a lot of the same emotions we do. When an elephant dies, the members of its herd and even other elephants who come across the body grieve and show respect. Elephants even shed tears of sadness during these times. They have a similar life span, they have empathy, and they understand the importance of teamwork. One thing I've found extremely inspiring is the fact that elephants don't get cancer. Because of this discovery, scientists are researching ways to cure cancer by creating a synthetic cancer-fighting protein based on a protein found in the blood of elephants.

Elephants, crystals, meditation, yoga, mindfulness, awareness, consciousness, law of attraction—these are all the things I'm becoming completely passionate about. In the process, I've made so many incredible discoveries about my own life and my purpose.

One way I can describe this enlightenment I've been given is to imagine I am a tree. I'm rooted, and I'm grounded. In the beginning of my life as a tree, I was given a camera with just one lens. This one lens served me well. It did the job, and I was able to capture beautiful pictures of the scenery in front of me. There are mountains to the right and a field of flowers, and to the left I see a cluster of tall buildings. However, with this particular lens, I'm only able to capture the scenery in portions. It doesn't zoom in or out, and since I'm a tree, I can't move closer or further away. So, in a sense, I can only view the scenery in one particular way. Sure, I can adjust the shutter speed or aperture, but the pictures will always come out somewhat the same.

Then, suddenly, I'm made aware of all the other lenses available. I didn't know any others existed. I try out the macro lens, and I'm astonished by the new perspective. Now I can get up close and personal with the flowers, and I see all the intricate details I never saw before. I see the veins in the petals and the curvature of the leaves. Then I try out a wide-angle lens, and now I can capture the entire scenery with just one picture.

This is what it feels like. I'm seeing the world in a whole new way, and it's absolutely breathtaking. It's a beauty I've never known before.

Notes

1. Gay Hendricks, *The Big Leap* (New York: HarperOne, 2009), 18.
2. Wayne W. Dyer, "Open Your Mind," *Dr. Wayne W. Dyer*, accessed December 14, 2018, https://www.drwaynedyer.com/blog/open-your-mind.
3. "How to Receive Signs from the Universe," *Gabby*, 2015, https://gabbybernstein.com/receive-signs-universe/#close-modal.

Chapter 7

So Much to Do, So Little Time

For as long as I can remember, I've been obsessed with routines, schedules, notepads, and day planners. The earliest I remember creating my own schedule was when I was in the third grade. I remember writing out my daily routine and placing it on my neatly made bed. I was kind of a perfectionist. I liked things organized and tidy even as a nine-year-old girl.

Motherhood has taught me *so* much about time management. I quickly learned that my idea of a perfect routine and clean house was not going to be the reality. I'm constantly having to adapt to new routines and schedules.

Although I've had a goal to write a book for over a decade, I'm actually really grateful this opportunity came along now and not sooner. My views on time management and so many other things have changed drastically over the last thirteen years since becoming a mom. I actually feel more equipped to write this book now, after acquiring a few more years of life experience. I've had all this time to try a million different ways to manage my time, figuring out what works and what doesn't. Ten years ago, my book concept was going to be solely based on time management; now I'm writing the book and only including a single chapter about time management. I've realized that time management and balance requires so much more than clear-cut instructions you can add to your to-do list. It requires refinement as a person in all aspects of life.

The struggle is real, my friends. I never truly understood the need for MORE time until I became a mother.

So much to do, so little time.

> It's not that we have too little time to do all the things we need to do, it is that we feel the need to do too many things in the time we have.[1]

For years I kept piling so much on my plate, feeling like I was running a race, never keeping up with all I thought was required to be a "good" mom.

People often ask me how I get so much done each day. Each year, my answer changes slightly. In the beginning, I would say, "Just cut out a few hours of sleep, and you'll be able to do it all too." A few years later, I would answer, "Do a little bit of EVERYTHING each day." Fast forward to NOW, and here is my advice.

It has only been recently that I've discovered a whole new approach to time management. As I've talked about in most of the chapters thus far, it all starts with the mind. Earlier in my life, I was prone to thinking overwhelming, undeserving thoughts, like *I'll never be as good as that other mom over there*, or *I should be doing this and more of that.*

Recently I heard someone say she wanted to stop *should*ing on herself. She was constantly telling herself all the things she SHOULD be doing until she finally realized that it's not about what we should be doing; it's about what we want to do, what we feel inspired to do, what feels like love, and what gives us purpose and fulfillment.

Whenever I'm feeling overwhelmed, I remind myself that I don't HAVE to do anything. I get to CHOOSE whether I do something. Nobody is making me do anything I don't genuinely want to do. There are no *shoulds*; there are only desires.

I just got done reading *The ONE Thing* by Gary Keller and Jay Papasan, and I was enlightened by their approach to balance. We are all seeking balance. We imagine balance to be total and complete serenity, a feeling that we are succeeding in all areas of our lives. But really when you think of what balance looks like visually, it's being in the middle, not on the outer edges. Being in the middle, balancing everything just perfectly, doesn't allow you to go "all in" on any one thing. Gary teaches that things balance out over time. Sometimes we need to put a little more time and energy into one thing for a while in order to get big results.[2]

As we strive to balance work and life, it's important that we recognize that our personal lives, family, and overall spiritual and mental well-being take precedence over anything else we have going on in our careers, meaning you can't go "all in" on your business if your health is at risk. For example, working night after night without getting the rest you need, skipping your exercise routine, living on caffeine and fast food, or underestimating the power of mind work and spiritual connection.

I like the way Stephen R. Covey demonstrates this. Imagine you have about five big rocks and a cup of sand. The big rocks represent God, family, health, and your spiritual well-being. The sand represents everything else. If you were to pour the sand into a jar first, then place the rocks on top, you'd discover that it won't all fit and it's completely overflowing. But if you place the rocks in first and then pour in the sand, it's amazing how everything suddenly fits.[3]

Remember your priorities when striving to reach big goals. Big accomplishments require massive amounts of energy. You need energy to be productive and to catapult you into action, so it's important to do the things that create energy for you. Make them a priority.

Some things, like sleep, exercise, eating right, and mental and spiritual development cannot be put on the back burner. So many of us moms are forfeiting sleep and healthy eating in an attempt to get it all done. We think we can get by without taking care of our bodies and our minds, but the truth is that it's absolutely impossible long-term. Eventually, you will run yourself into the ground, and at that point it can be extremely hard to pick yourself up and start again.

Multitasking is a way of life for us mamas. We discover the power of multitasking right away—doing laundry while listening to podcasts, walking on the treadmill while reading a book, helping kids with homework while preparing dinner, and the list goes on.

In most cases, multitasking is brilliant! But when it comes to tasks that require focus, like reading, writing, creating, and connecting, multitasking isn't necessarily a good idea. There have been multiple studies done on the effectiveness of multitasking.[4] Come to find out, it's not always a good thing. Yes, it works when one thing you're doing is practically second nature and doesn't require much brain energy. But sometimes multitasking can be a huge time suck—like when you're trying to write a book and email notifications keep popping up, your phone dings with a new text message, or one of your kids comes in, needing a snack.

Every time I break away to check an email or text or attend to my children, I'm actually extending the time it takes to do the task. Every time I get distracted, it takes a certain amount of time for my brain to refocus on the task at hand.

I've learned how important it is to turn off all notifications and protect my writing time by either waking up early before the kids or getting a babysitter to take care of the kids while I get some uninterrupted time to write and create.

When it comes to managing our time most effectively, it all starts with the habits we've created for ourselves. For example, a good morning routine is a great place to start when trying to incorporate useful habits. Research backs the idea that mornings are an optimal time to create, be productive, and focus. If you can start your morning off right, it will set the tone for the rest of the day. Back to the rocks and sand concept. Start with the big, important rocks FIRST, and then everything else will just fall into place.

Creating habits is another important part of time management. The more good habits you develop, the more effective and productive you will become. The thought of creating habits always sounds a little daunting at first because we know it requires a lot of time and discipline, but the awesome thing about habits is they only require discipline in the beginning. Once it becomes a habit, you don't even need to think about it or try to do it—you just do it with little to no effort.

The important thing to remember when trying to create habits is you MUST start extremely small to achieve big results. For example, as I'm getting closer to the big 4-0, I'm beginning to notice my muscles aren't as firm as they were when I was in my twenties.

I admit, I don't work out very hard. I've been considerably consistent with my daily exercising, and it is practically a habit for me, but I don't really push myself hard. I mostly walk for twenty or thirty minutes, and that's about it. I haven't really done any strength training for over a year.

Recently, I decided I needed to start toning up a bit. Instead of making big goals to work out an extra hour each day or start attending a bunch of intense fitness classes, I decided to start small. I went to Pinterest, found the easiest thirty-day challenge, and printed it out. Basically, all it requires me to do each day is less than five minutes' worth of simple exercises like squats, push-ups, and leg lifts. Each day, the number gradually increases, but overall, the time required is totally doable for anyone.

I started doing this thirty-day challenge simply to create a habit of doing strength training, not necessarily for results at this point. Five minutes a day for thirty days is not going to create noticeable results in muscle tone, but the result I'm looking for is the habit. Little by little, a little becomes a lot. As I make this a new habit, not only will I gradually see slight changes in my body, but one year from now, if I maintain consistency, I will be a changed person. And that is ultimately the goal—to create habits that help me evolve and become a better me, whether the results are outwardly noticeable or not.

Here's a little rundown of what my ideal typical week looks like.

Monday

I like to start the week off by going to the grocery store, starting a few loads of laundry, and doing a little meal prep. I don't work at all on Mondays. I try to focus only on my homemaking responsibilities, homework, and family time.

Tuesday

This is the day that I usually get a babysitter to take over for me while I lock myself in my room or office to bang out some writing or video editing. I have a goal to create one YouTube video, blog post, and podcast episode each week. Tuesdays I work on my to-do list, create my YouTube video, and write my blog post or podcast outline.

Wednesday

Wednesday morning, I have no kids at home for a couple hours since my youngest is now in preschool twice a week. During that time, I record my podcast episode, edit it, and publish it.

Thursday

Again, my youngest is at school, so for a couple hours I work on any remaining items on my to-do list and send out my newsletter. Now I'm officially done working for the week, and I try to sign off of everything else until Tuesday again. The rest of the weekend is all family time—although I do spend about an hour each day on social media posting something and engaging on my friends' feeds.

Friday

This is the day I try to tie up any loose ends and gradually begin letting go of it all. This is not easy for me to do. I get obsessive-compulsive about work and getting things done. I have to force myself to slow down and stop everything to be present, relax, play, and just have fun.

Saturday

Saturday mornings I spend a little time planning out my week, doing a little writing, getting house chores done, and going on a little run outside. Then the rest of the day is playtime, which I spend entertaining my kids and their friends.

Sunday

Sunday has always been the hardest day for me. I like the idea of resting and relaxing, but when I actually try to do it, my mind goes crazy thinking about all the things I should be doing. I'm getting better at this over time, but it's something I make a priority because I believe in the power of pause, rest, and relaxation. It's the best way to end a busy week and regenerate enough to power through another productive week.

I would also like to share my morning routine because this routine is actually the most important part of my day. I created a free morning routine download on my blog. You can go to www.wannabebalanced.com/morning-routine if you'd like to print out a few copies to serve as a guide for you.

Morning Routine

Lately, I've been extremely absorbed in the practice of meditation. I'd wanted to make time for it for years but totally underestimated its value in my life. I didn't realize how essential it is to quiet the mind, focus on the breath, and visualize. Check out my YouTube playlist on meditation for video tours of my meditation stations, as well as some other helpful information when it comes to contemplation, reflection, and manifestation. Go to www.wannabebalanced.com/youtubemeditation.

When I had my "faith crisis" (see chapter six) is when I finally began taking meditation seriously. It became essential; the only way to calm my overwhelming anxiety was to meditate. I had to separate myself from my mind and realign with my true self. What I've come to realize is that we are not our minds. We believe that our thoughts make up who we are, but that is simply not true. There is a difference between what the mind offers and what the spirit offers. When we can get quiet and practice the art of separating ourselves from the mind to the point of connecting to our inner being, our spirit, God, the universe—whatever you want to call it—that's when we discover a whole new level of peace and enlightenment.

Every morning, and I'm serious when I say *every* morning, I look forward to retreating to my zen den, lighting some candles or incense, putting in my headphones, and getting lost in the peaceful meditation sounds on Pandora. Sometimes I use apps or YouTube videos to guide me through meditation, but mostly I start by relaxing my whole body, focusing on my breathing, and turning off the thoughts. It's not easy to turn off the mind, and that's why it's important to focus on your breathing and relaxing different areas of your body. I spend about ten minutes doing that, and then I take time to thank God and the universe for everything I have. After that, I visualize.

Visualization is my favorite part and what I believe really helps me the most. I visualize feeling peaceful and safe. I visualize exactly how I want my day to go, and I visualize my future. By doing this, I'm able to release my worries and trust that everything in my life is exactly the way it's supposed to be. I have an unlimited amount of time. There is no need to rush or hurry through life. There is no need to create never-ending to-do lists. I'm more present and trusting knowing that everything that needs to get done will be done in perfect timing.

It's pretty incredible how life changing this has been for me. I'm now operating at a much higher frequency. Some days I feel like I am literally floating through my day. Everything flows, my mind is calm, and I'm not thinking about what needs to get done; I'm just *doing* what needs to be done in the moment. I'm more aware, at peace, and overall more productive than ever before.

Notes

1. Gary Keller and Jay Papasan, *The ONE Thing: The Surprisingly Simple Truth behind Extraordinary Results* (Austin: Keller, 2003).
2. Keller and Papasan, *The ONE Thing.*

3. Stephen R. Covey, "Choices to Extraordinary Productivity," www.franklincovey.com.
4. For example, see Adam Gorlick, "Media Multitaskers Pay Mental Price, Stanford Study Shows," *Stanford News*, August 24, 2009, https://news.stanford.edu/news/2009/august24/multitask-research-study-082409.html.

Chapter 8

Overcoming Jealousy and Resentment

I was given about seven or eight months to write this book, so in order to get 'er done, I made a goal to write one chapter a week. I initially made a list of all the topics I wanted to write about and have been working down the list, creating chapters one topic at a time.

This week's topic couldn't have come at a better time. Although I've written about this theme multiple times on my blog and have learned and overcome so much, jealousy and resentment continue to haunt me every now and again. It just goes to show that some lessons take a lifetime to master.

I think jealousy and resentment go hand in hand because first we experience jealousy, and usually it's followed by a bit of resentment toward the person we are jealous of or toward the life we've been dealt. Sometimes we want to blame others or our circumstances for our not having everything we desire.

As a teenager, I experienced a lot of jealousy. I was jealous of other girls who I thought were prettier than me, skinnier than me, had cuter clothes than me, and had more friends than me. In junior high, I didn't believe I was all that smart or pretty—just average. I had fine hair, acne, crooked teeth we couldn't afford to fix, chicken legs, big feet (what my dad jokingly called "skis"), and I wore unsightly hand-me-down clothes because we never had money to buy new ones. It didn't help that I was constantly moving into a new school every six months and being forever labeled as the new kid on the block.

In ninth grade, after switching schools yet again, I remember the horror I felt that first day walking into the lunchroom and not knowing a single person. I didn't want to look like a loser and sit by myself, but I didn't have the guts to go up to people I didn't know and simply ask if I could sit with them. For that reason, I took my lunch into the bathroom and ate it alone in a stall. It sounds completely unsanitary, I know, but low self-esteem and self-consciousness can make you do crazy things.

I felt like high school was a breeding ground for jealousy, and at that age it's very difficult to bridle it. I didn't know what to do with the emotion other than suffer. I didn't know it was my own thoughts that were subjecting me to inner turmoil.

As I've gotten older, I've learned how to handle jealousy a little better, but it definitely still haunts me at times. You know that moment you're feeling so good about your life and everything you've created up until now? Then you hop on social media and get to peek inside the lives of others. Your friend announces she's pregnant when you've been trying for years. A colleague of yours gets the promotion or business deal you were working for. Your neighbor gets a new car, a new kitchen, or even a new house! You see pictures of amazing vacations while you're sitting there with spit-up and snot all over your shirt and feeling too fat to wear a swimsuit since you're still trying to lose the baby weight. Suddenly, the beautiful, abundant life you built doesn't seem so glamorous anymore.

Social media is a blessing and a curse. The answer is not to abandon social media altogether, but to learn a lesson about jealousy. How can we overcome our envious natures? How can we stay in a place of peace and love for everyone? Those are the big questions. I've found plenty of tips and advice on the matter, but I tell ya, it's no easy task.

It's human nature to want what others have. We recognize it in our own children as early as age two. They are happily playing with a particular toy until their sibling walks in with a different toy. Suddenly they must have *that* toy! The one they have just doesn't seem as cool anymore. The psychology around it is when someone else has something, it only SEEMS to be better than what we have because we don't have it. In other words, the grass always seems greener until we get there and realize it's really not—it just *looks* greener from a distance.

Whenever I feel jealousy, instead of judging myself for feeling this way, I've learned to simply approach it with curiosity. I ask myself a list of questions.

Do I REALLY Want What They Have?

Sometimes I look at others and think I want what they have, but when it comes down to it, I wonder, *Do I really?* Everything comes with a price, and it may be a price I'm not willing to pay.

Let's take celebrities, for example. Just like we have celebrities in this world, there are also "celebrities" within smaller niche organizations and businesses. In our Isagenix business, there are definitely people we deem as celebrities. Sean and I have been in Isagenix since practically the beginning. At one point, we were the youngest millionaires within the company, which means we held "celebrity status" for a moment. Since then, the company has grown, and so has the amount of people who have achieved high rankings. This means that little by little, Sean and I have become just another successful distributor among hundreds of others. We no longer stand out among the crowd and much more is required in order to be featured, recognized, or even asked to be keynote speakers at the company's live events.

We've never really been bothered by this, mainly because we know what it would take on our end to be back on stage. We decided early on that our goal was to have freedom with our time. We wanted just enough money to live a comfortable lifestyle without having to work long hours like we did in the beginning. We didn't want to travel all over, attending every event—not because we don't love and respect the power of attending those events, but because we didn't want to leave the kids while they were young.

Like I said, you need to ask yourself if it's a price you're willing to pay.

Am I Practicing Gratitude?

Sometimes it's just a matter of switching the focus from what I don't have to all the amazing things I DO have. It's easy to get caught up in noticing all that I want, and the fact that I don't have it yet is enough to send me down a path of resentment. I simply take out a piece of paper and start writing down everything I have, and before long I'm feeling a flood of gratitude for the abundance of blessings God has given me. I list everything, even down to the clean air I breathe and all the functioning organs I have that make up a healthy, physically capable body.

Becoming ungrateful and discontent can easily take over my thoughts if I'm not consciously managing them. I have big goals in business and blogging, and I'm constantly striving to reach new heights. Sometimes all I can see are the people who have achieved more than me or are doing it better in every way. I easily forget how far I've come on my own journey.

> In the hopes of reaching the moon men fail to see the flowers that blossom at their feet.
>
> —Albert Schweitzer

One of my favorite talks by Dieter F. Uchtdorf is his "Forget Me Not" message. I highly recommend reading it over and over. He eloquently put into words the feelings I've been experiencing. He compares our tendency to be discontent in life to the classic *Charlie and the Chocolate Factory* story. In the beginning, everyone was so concerned with getting the golden ticket that even the candy bar itself was no longer enjoyable.

> This is not to say that we should abandon hope or temper our goals. Never stop striving for the best that is within you. Never stop hoping for all of the righteous desires of your heart. But don't close your eyes and hearts to the simple and elegant beauties of each day's ordinary moments that make up a rich, well-lived life.
>
> —Dieter F. Uchtdorf[1]

Is It Because I Feel like Their Success Means There's Less for Me?

Jealousy only happens when we have a scarcity mentality about things—thinking that because someone else has something we want, there is less of it for me. What I've come to realize and continue to remind myself of is that there is more than enough to go around. There is an abundance of good things just waiting to come my way. God or the universe is always conspiring in my favor. Everything that was meant to come to me will come, and if I'm constantly looking for the good, then I will realize just how blessed I am and how abundantly the blessings continue to flow into my life.

Do I Resent Others Because They Are Successfully Living Their Dreams When I Am Not?

Jealousy can also be triggered when we see someone else living their dream. It reminds us of the fact that we either gave up or never really tried to pursue ours. It can be an indicator of something you should or want to be doing.

Who Am I Competing With?

I read an interesting explanation of the human competitive nature from the book *Status Anxiety*:

> It is the feeling that we might, under different circumstances, be something other than what we are—a feeling inspired by exposure to the superior achievements of those whom we take to be our equals—that generates anxiety and resentment. If we are short, say but live among people of our same height, we will not be unduly troubled by questions of size. But if others in our group grow just a little taller than us, we are liable to feel sudden unease and to be gripped by dissatisfaction and envy, even though we have not ourselves diminished in size by so much as a fraction of a millimeter.
>
> Given the vast inequalities we are daily confronted with, the most notable feature of envy may be that we manage not to envy everyone. There are people whose enormous blessings leave us wholly untroubled, even as others' negligible advantages become a source of relentless torment for us. We envy only those whom we feel ourselves to be like—we envy only members of our reference group. There are few successes more unendurable than those of our ostensible equals.
>
> —Alain de Botton[2]

It's interesting to ponder the competitive nature of man. We tend to lose sight of the ultimate competition—self-competition.

You see, our competitiveness was not meant to be used against each other; it was designed to be used against ourselves. Our goal should be to become better than the person we were yesterday, and that's it!

This reminds me of some pages I marked in a book called *Girl Code*, and it's a message I hope all women will heed whenever they find themselves feeling jealous and withholding information, support, and love because of our insecurities.

> There is no reason to hoard information, connections, or insight. Wisdom is meant to be shared, so let's start sharing what we've learned to make each other better. Let's start building each other up. . . .
>
> Women need to learn to empower one another, not tear them down. If you see a beautiful woman, tell her. If a woman is being a great mother, tell her. Wearing cool shoes? Tell her. Lost weight and looks great? Tell her. There is more than enough success and happiness to go around. The universal laws of abundance prove that there is absolutely no reason to compete. Competition is soooo '90s. Evolve past it and learn to collaborate instead.[3]

This was so beautifully said, and I'm passionate about the importance of learning to love and support all women.

Am I Comparing My Starting Point with Someone Else's End, or Their Strengths to My Weaknesses?

Over time, I have learned to be inspired by the success of other women. I've also learned that being happy for someone else's success doesn't mean that there is less opportunity for me—it simply shows me what's possible. If she can do it, then so can I.

> The people you think are perfect are not. And yet we spend so much time and energy comparing ourselves to others—usually

> comparing our weaknesses to their strengths. This drives us to create expectations for ourselves that are impossible to meet. As a result, we never celebrate our good efforts because they seem to be less than what someone else does.
>
> —Dieter F. Uchtdorf[4]

We compare ourselves so much and tend to feel resentment toward people who seem to be happier or more successful than we are. When I began blogging over nine years ago, I thought of it as a way to record and share publicly the experiences and life lessons I was learning. I started out with so much excitement and direction; I felt like I was fulfilling a special mission, and it gave me purpose.

Over time, I lost sight of my purpose, and blogging became a competition. I suddenly found myself feeling inferior to all these other amazing bloggers. I compared myself so much to their beautiful pictures and perfectly written blog posts that I felt I didn't measure up. I went through major self-doubt and lacked the confidence I had when I first started. I began telling myself it was just a waste of time because I didn't have anything different or unique to offer. Everything had already been said or done before. So I gave up. I quit blogging for a few years.

Really, it's all about shifting our focus. We have to pay attention to all the gifts, talents, and blessings that *we* have. Each one of us is unique and wonderfully made. We are all loved equally by God; there are no favorites. Also, we have to remember that nobody has it all. It may look like it on social media, but we have to remember the reality of life. We all have struggles, we all have weaknesses, and we all suffer from pain, loss, and disappointment.

Do You Think They Are Better than You?

I used to have the belief that other people were simply born better than me. If they were prettier, that meant they were better; if they were skinnier, that meant they were happier. If they were wealthy, that meant they were smarter and had been given more opportunity. I've only recently begun to grasp our infinite potential. Everyone is capable of incredible achievements and astounding growth.

Are You Forgetting Who's in Charge?

Sometimes we beg and plead with God to give us what we want, but there are many times we don't get what we want. It's not because we aren't deserving of everything we want; instead, we may not be ready for it. Just as you can't force a flower to grow faster than nature intends, we can't force things to happen in our lives if we aren't ready. We may need to learn a few more things through our struggles. We don't learn by getting everything we want exactly when we want it.

I remember back in high school when I started dating different guys. I would get in a relationship, and then eventually we'd break up. I was heartbroken every time and wished so badly it didn't end.

Only in hindsight can I recognize God's perfect plan for me. Now I'm aware there was much more in store for me—things I didn't foresee and couldn't even imagine were possible.

Other Reasons We Feel Resentment

- We didn't get invited to the party.
- We don't feel supported by friends or family members.
- We feel we've been taken advantage of.
- We feel frustrated that a friend chooses to be our competition instead of working together in business.
- Someone is spreading rumors about us.
- We are being left out, we're not included in a group of friends, or we see a picture on social media of our friends hanging out, *and we're not in it.*

The first step to overcoming these negative emotions is to get it all out. This feeling is like an infection in the body. You need to get it out, so SAY what you're feeling or thinking. Say it or write it. Just don't say it *to* anyone, and be sure to rip up the paper and throw it away once you're done. You can be as mean and vicious as you want because nobody can hear it. The purpose is to remove the negativity, not hurt anyone. Our knee-jerk reaction is to hurt someone back when they have hurt us, but this won't solve anything.

The next step is to write out your own weaknesses. It's good to establish some humility in this kind of situation and not be the victim. Take responsibility for your own mistakes. Recognize that you're not perfect either. You may have done this very thing to someone else; simply recognize that we all have things we need to work on.

Ignorance Is Bliss

Now tell your brain what you want to hear. You can choose to believe whatever you want to believe, so create the perfect scenario in your mind. Come up with an explanation for the person's actions. What might have caused the person to do this? Have compassion toward them. Understand that they are probably doing the best they know how. Maybe the person that hurt you has legitimate issues that caused them to do what they did. There's got to be a reason, and you can create whatever reason you want. The goal is to feel better, and it's okay to tell your mind what it wants to hear. Ignorance is bliss, and la-la land is grand.

More often than not, we actually create stories in our own minds that aren't even true, which causes us to suffer, so you need to create a better story. You didn't get invited to the party—what are you making that mean? Most the time, we are gathering up evidence and creating a story that proves we are unloved or unappreciated. We make other people's actions, or lack of actions, mean something negative about us. So stop! And recreate the story.

Now FORGIVE!

I can honestly say when I practice these steps that I feel a hundred times better. I put in the time and effort, then ask God for guidance, and usually I'm led to the right resources that help me overcome the negative feelings.

The final thing we must remember is that the feeling of jealousy is totally optional. It doesn't just suddenly happen to us without any control on our end. We absolutely have control over whether or not we feel jealous, because it all comes down to the thoughts in our heads. Instead of looking at other people and thinking their lives are better, we can redirect our attention and remind ourselves of at least five things we love about US or our lives, and make this a habit.

Notes

1. Dieter F. Uchtdorf, "Forget Me Not," *Ensign*, Nov. 2011.
2. Alain de Botton, *Status Anxiety* (New York: Random House, 2004), 26–27.
3. Cara Alwill Leyba, *Girl Code* (Passionista Publishing, 2015), back cover, 17.
4. Dieter F. Uchtdorf, "Forget Me Not," *Ensign*, Nov. 2011.

Chapter 9

Should I Have Another Baby?

Did you know elephants are pregnant for twenty-two months? What?! I can't even imagine what that would be like.

There was a season when I was either pregnant or nursing for six consecutive years. Exactly a year after having my fourth child, I decided to get my tubes tied. The pregnancy and childbirth were still very much fresh in my mind. I was sleep-deprived, overwhelmed, and flat-out exhausted. I also felt a bit resentful because I was up in the middle of the night breastfeeding while my husband and his worthless nipples slept peacefully.

It was then that I decided NO MORE. I couldn't imagine doing this all over again. So I made the appointment to get the tubal ligation surgery. I was 100 percent positive this was what I wanted to do. My husband, Sean, was fine either way. He understood that this was mostly my decision to make and supported me no matter what.

The day of the surgery, I remember the nurse asking me again if I was sure this was what I wanted and explained that this procedure was permanent. I enthusiastically replied, "YES!"

I was excited about the idea of not having to take birth control pills or deal with IUD side effects, and I was completely ready to move into the next chapter of my life.

I daydreamed of the days when there would be no more diaper bags full of everything but the kitchen sink, no more heavy strollers to lift in and out of my car or complicated car seats to strap my kids into, nights where I would finally get to *sleep*, and peaceful hours when the kids were in school all day. Oh, the life I would lead . . . There were so many things that this mama heart desired to do, and I felt so overwhelmed and burned out by the many demands of motherhood.

The day after my surgery, I panicked. Reality set in, and I suddenly realized I was officially *done* having babies. That night, I cried myself to sleep. I was shocked that I felt such sadness and a tinge of regret about the decision I had made.

As the days passed, I got over it and moved on . . . *or so I thought.*

Two years later, I found myself feeling deeply saddened over the fact that my baby was no longer a baby. He was now three, potty trained, and becoming more independent each day. The only thing keeping me from having a complete meltdown was the fact that I was still nursing him. I knew that I needed to wean him soon but couldn't bring myself to let go of the last piece of babyhood. I was going on a total of seven years straight pregnant or nursing, and at this point I was feeling quite proud of myself. Did you know that elephants believe in extended nursing too? They, too, nurse their babies for three to four years.

I started jokingly telling Sean that we should get my tubes reattached. Then we would both laugh it off and remind ourselves of my sleepless nights and resentment toward Sean because of it. He still remembers the look of disgust I regularly gave him as he awoke from a restful night's sleep, and how I frequently lashed out any time he dared say he was tired. Men have no idea what "tired" means.

Although I remembered all the hard parts, I couldn't stop thinking about it. I began researching the reversal surgery and felt a bit excited about the possibility. Then I presented the idea to Sean once again. This time he realized I was serious, so we had a good long talk about it and started exploring our options.

We set up two consultations just to get different opinions and find out as much about the procedure as possible. The first doctor looked at the operation report from my tubal ligation and expressed his lack of hope for a positive outcome. You see, there are different ways of getting your tubes tied. This was news to me, but I took full responsibility. I never imagined I would be in this situation in the first place; therefore, I didn't take the time to look into the different ways of having this surgery done.

I found out that my tubes were cauterized instead of clamped. This means that a good portion of my tubes were simply burned, making them very difficult to re-attach because there was little to work with. The doctor recommended in vitro fertilization because the chances of the tubal reversal surgery being successful were extremely low, not to mention the surgery itself is pretty pricey, and of course they don't offer any kind of money-back guarantee.

The second doctor said the same thing, but she seemed to have a little more hope for the outcome of the reversal. She had only done a handful of surgeries that were similar to my case, and she said that a couple of them were successful. I was very emotional at this point. In between sobs, I was able to get the information I needed but left feeling extremely discouraged.

Together, Sean and I decided that we did *not* want to go through the long and emotional process of doing in vitro and would take our chances on the reversal surgery. (I documented portions of this whole process on YouTube and created a video playlist if any of you would like to get a real-life look into our journey.)

I went into the surgery with high hopes but still open to the fact that it may not work. As I was waking up from anesthesia, before I could even open my eyes, I was mumbling, "Did it work?" The nurse explained that I would have to talk to the doctor to find out how the surgery went. The suspense was killing me, and I kept pestering the nurse to give me some kind of answer. He had nothing, so I began demanding to see my husband. At the same time, I was suddenly hit with an intense amount of pain. The nurse gave me another dose of morphine and brought me out to Sean.

The first thing I said to him was, "What did the doctor say?" He wasn't concerned with explaining the results to me just yet; he wanted to make sure I was okay because the nurse had notified him I was crying in pain. He kept asking me how I was doing, and I kept asking him to tell me what the doctor said. Finally, he explained that the surgery was *somewhat* successful. Meaning I now had *one* working tube. Unfortunately, the other tube was irreparable.

"One working tube?" I said. "That's good, right? Is it possible to get pregnant with one tube?" He reassured me that it was very much possible, and I broke down in tears of relief.

Now here I am, one year post-surgery and still not pregnant. As the months have passed, I've found myself feeling a roller-coaster of emotions. First I was excited about the potential of having another baby. Every month, the anticipation was thrilling but was met with yet another letdown.

I'm even back to the point I was at when I got my tubes tied in the first place. I've been second-guessing everything and feeling so confused. I'm suddenly afraid of doing the baby thing all over again.

As I write this chapter, it's early morning in Lake Powell, Arizona. I'm here with my little family, staying in a charming little cottage we rented. I'm realizing this is our first time coming to Lake Powell because we are finally in a stage that we CAN. All our kids are older, and they're great swimmers. Sean and I are getting a glimpse into how fun this new season of our lives can be. Instead of regretting getting my tubes tied, now I find myself regretting that I got the reversal—even hoping that I don't get pregnant.

Wallowing in my own confusion, I ask myself, *What was all this for?* Was I even inspired by God to get the reversal surgery, or was this just me panicking and worrying about never having another baby and struggling to accept change and welcome a new season? What does it all mean?

As human beings, we have a deep desire to find meaning in our lives, circumstances, and choices we make. We want to know why.

> Suffering ceases to be suffering at the moment it finds a meaning.
>
> —Viktor Frankl[1]

Do you feel as overwhelmed as I do after reading my story? My purpose in sharing this is not to validate the indulgent emotion we call confusion but to help you see that we all struggle with it. As I struggle to overcome my own confusion around this, I'm reminded of a couple messages I've heard in the past.

One of my favorite messages by Jeffrey R. Holland is called "Wrong Roads." It's a story of when he and his son set out on a scenic drive and found themselves lost right before sundown. They stopped and said a prayer, trying to figure out which way to go. Holland describes the moment as follows:

> I asked my son to pray about which road to take, and he felt strongly that we should go to the right, and I did as well. We went to the right, and it was a dead end. We went about five hundred yards, and it was an absolute dead end, clearly the wrong road. Turned around came back out, took the other road, and clearly to the left was the correct road. Somewhere along the way, Matt said, "Dad, why did we feel after praying about it that the right road was the correct one to take, and it wasn't?"
>
> I said, "I think that the Lord, His wish for us there and His answer to our prayer was to get us on the right road as quickly as possible. With some reassurance, with some understanding that we were on the right road and we didn't have to worry about it. And in this case, the easiest way to do that was to let us go a little ways on the wrong road and very quickly know without a doubt that it was the wrong road, and therefore know with equal certainty, with equal conviction that the other one was the right road."[2]

I love this message because it reminds me that God has unique ways of steering us in the right direction. He's always guiding us and helping us get on the right road as quickly as possible, allowing us to make our own choices, and encouraging us to keep going even when things don't always make sense.

Sitting in indecision is a waste of time. It's important to give yourself time to think about your options, but not sit in confusion, going back and forth on your decision. Establish a verdict and go for it. If it turns out to be the wrong choice, ultimately it wasn't the wrong choice because now you're back on track with even more conviction than before. I'm beginning to understand that there really are no wrong decisions because either one you take will lead you to the right road eventually. Even if it means taking the scenic route in order to learn what you needed to learn.

In my case, I think I'm learning that I don't have to feel regret either way. Feeling regret is a choice, and it's all based on the thoughts I choose to have about my choices.

Jody Moore says, "When we worry about making the right choice, it's always based on our desire to feel good in the future. Or to avoid feeling regret. The way to ensure that we feel good in the future is to remember that your feelings come from your thoughts, and we get to choose what we want to think about our circumstance. The feelings we have won't be because we had a baby or didn't have a baby. It will be because of what we're thinking about it."[3]

Isn't this absolutely liberating? No more worrying about doing everything exactly right. Just live life, take risks, try new things, experiment, and learn as you go. Confusion is a choice. We choose to be confused by simply saying, "I'm confused," or "I don't know." Just trust your decision, and give yourself a break if it turns out to be the "wrong" one. Like I said, the wrong choice doesn't really exist because of the valuable lessons that lie within the sometimes longer journey of getting on the right road.

It's like when we advise our kids and our teenagers to make certain choices. They don't always want to do what we tell them to do and choose to learn something the hard way. But hard is good—it refines us and gets us closer to becoming who we are meant to be.

I was definitely the defiant teenager. My mom told me not to get in a serious relationship in high school. She warned me to stay away from alcohol. She encouraged me to remain close to God. She gave me all the right instructions to live a happy, safe, and joyful life.

Did I follow her instructions? NOPE! Was my mom sad about it? YEP! Any mother would be as she's having to watch her daughter suffer heartache and disappointment. Do I regret my choices? I regretted them when I was suffering through the sadness of a breakup. But now that I've overcome that tremendously difficult season, I don't regret it one bit. It was an essential part of my plan that made me who I am today—a much stronger woman with a greater appreciation of what real love and joy looks like.

Now that I'm married to someone who truly loves me and who is also loyal, an ambitious provider, amazing father, and an incredible husband, there are days I'm overwhelmed with gratitude that I was blessed with such a man in my life. I never would have truly understood how great my husband is if I hadn't experienced his opposites.

Again, this is a reminder that the wrong choice doesn't exist in the end. It will all come together exactly the way it was supposed to. We can't avoid pain or sorrow; they are an important part of life. We must experience the bad in order to appreciate the good. So stop choosing confusion, make a choice, and go with it!

You can always turn back; nothing is a waste of time. It is what it is, and you move on; you keep going. Our lives are great, big puzzles. The pieces by themselves make absolutely no sense, but little by little, as you connect the pieces, you begin to see a beautiful masterpiece. Trust that everything will all make sense in the end. You will find meaning in every choice, every mistake, and every detour.

It's the contrast of things that allows you to realize what you don't want, which provides you with clarity and the knowledge of what you do want in your life. So appreciate the opposition when you face it. It's all part of the internal navigation system we have within us, helping us get to our final destination. When we make a wrong turn, navigation simply says, "Rerouting." It will never lead you somewhere other than where you want to go. The destination always remains the same; it's just that sometimes we take a little detour.

Notes

1. Viktor E. Frankl, *Man's Search for Meaning* (Boston: Beacon Press, 1959).
2. "Wrong Roads," LDS Media Library, narrated by Jeffrey R. Holland, video.
3. Jody Moore, "Better Than Happy," Podcast Episode #116: Should You Have More Babies? Oct. 5, 2017.

Chapter 10

It's Not about YOU

You probably think this chapter is about you, don't you, don't you, don't you?

Sorry to burst your bubble, but this chapter is about me!

Here's a story. It's Mother's Day. *It's my day*, I think to myself. I lie in bed, waiting for my breakfast, because that's what happens on Mother's Day, right? It's the day where all worship my amazingness and treat me like royalty. After all, I did give birth four times, two of which were unmedicated.

I wait and wait. No breakfast. I finally get out of bed and go downstairs. Surely there's a gourmet meal all prepared, with Mother's Day cards, flowers, and gifts galore.

I enter the kitchen to see . . . nothing. There is no breakfast. There are no gifts and no cards. The only "gift" I can see is a sink full of dishes.

The day goes on, and I realize there is nothing remarkable planned. I try to hide my disappointment, but that's kind of impossible for me. Before long, things take a turn for the worse. I mope around feeling sorry for myself. *Why am I so unappreciated?* I think. My frustration becomes contagious, and by the end of the day, nobody's feeling joyful. Instead of simply relishing in this special day, I went into it with such high expectations that it was doomed from the beginning.

As mothers we envision exactly what we want from our family on Mother's Day, and sometimes we are left feeling a little disappointed—*at least that's been the case for me.* We want to be pampered, showered with gifts, brought breakfast in bed, and basically given a day off from motherhood duties. Most the time I do get treated pretty awesome, but every once in a while, I realize I set the bar pretty dang high.

This kind of thing has happened to me a few times in my life, not just on Mother's Day. It's happened on birthdays, anniversaries, and other special occasions, like the times I gave birth to a human! I've been guilty of putting myself so high on the pedestal that I practically expect to receive a World Cup trophy or something. Although I'm a mother, I've learned to acknowledge that Mother's Day is not about me. It's about focusing on all the mothers in my own life, and not waiting and hoping with high expectations that my husband or kids will treat me like the *queen* I am.

In our selfie-obsessed and somewhat narcissistic generation, we are seeing more and more anxiety and depression. In my opinion, in some cases, anxiety and depression can be triggered by focusing too much on ourselves. By constantly scrutinizing how we compare to others and dwelling on how our flaws are on display for everyone to see and judge us, we fall into the subconscious idea that the world revolves around us, and that is a heavy burden to bear.

One thing I'm really trying to get through my head is that everything is not about ME! As spiritual beings having a human experience, we are constantly fighting against the tendencies of the natural man. In our efforts to discover ourselves by studying personal development and taking time for self-care, we can create an accidental self-absorbed reality.

This is especially true as we go through our adolescent years. Our minds our consumed with questions such as *How do I look?*

What should I wear? I wonder what they think of me, Am I popular? or *Am I pretty/fun/smart/awesome?* Everything people do and say becomes all about us.

It's Not about You . . .

I'm realizing how great of a mantra this can be in every situation we find ourselves in. It's not about YOU! It sounds so harsh and, at the same time, absolutely liberating! If you think about it, this statement literally removes you from the egotistical state of mind.

What people say . . . it's not about you. It's their opinion based on their beliefs, backgrounds, personalities, and preferences. Have you ever wondered why some people absolutely ADORE you and others want nothing to do with you? Well, it's because what they are thinking and the words they are choosing to express themselves with have absolutely everything to do with them and the way THEY perceive you.

What people do . . . it's not about you. For example, let's say your friend decides to plan a girls' trip and doesn't invite you. The only reason this might hurt is that you make it mean something about YOU. Maybe she forgot to include you, maybe she assumed you couldn't go, or maybe she just needs some alone time with a particular friend. It doesn't have to mean anything negative about you and your likability as a friend.

How people respond . . . it's not about you. Maybe they are having a bad day, or maybe even a good day. If they are all giddy and excited about something you did or said, it has everything to do with the thoughts they are choosing. So don't let it go to your head—haha. You're great and all, but your greatness isn't defined by the opinions and reactions of others.

When your spouse says or does something you don't like . . . it's not about you. I've definitely gotten really good at not taking my husband's actions personally. I can't make my husband angry or even happy. Only his thoughts about the circumstance have the ability to do that. Usually when I turn things around and put myself in his shoes I can better understand where he is coming from, and it becomes clear that his actions or words are not personal.

When you create value and put it out into the world . . . it's not about you. It's about serving, uplifting, and inspiring others. It's not about how you look, how eloquently you deliver the message, or what people think of you. It's about the goal of making a positive impact, not about how amazing you are because of what you created.

When you serve others . . . it's not about you. It's about using your gifts to better the lives of other people. This mentality allows us to stop obsessing over whether we're good enough or worthy enough. We simply go to work creating, loving, teaching, and serving. When you give your all and surrender the outcome, then you experience true joy and purpose.

When you're parenting your children . . . it's not about you. It's not about how you are seen as a mother. It's about teaching, loving, and nurturing—not with the hope and expectation others will say what a great mother you are, or even that one day your own kids will acknowledge or appreciate all you did for them, because they may never fully appreciate your sacrifices and effort. Again, it's not about you.

We can even take it a step further and decide that even our own birthdays are not about us. We can think of it instead as a day to express gratitude for life; a day to thank our parents for deciding to bring us into this world.

When we stop making everything about us, we realize how much sweeter this life can be.

Stop *Shoulding* on Others

*Should*ing is when we sit around waiting for others to fulfill our needs or do what we think they *should* be doing according to our manuals—the manuals that we've completely made up in our own minds. They may not have any validity whatsoever; they're just a made-up list of *should*. My spouse should pick up his shoes, my kids should be grateful, my friends should invite me to everything, my mom should call me more, my dad should be more responsible, etc.

We're so good at *should*ing on others. We even *should* ourselves too. We have high expectations of what we *should* be doing instead of appreciating the things we *do* accomplish, especially all the things we have done and overcome.

I've noticed that when I spend time in nature and become aware of the beautiful scenery, I feel a huge sense of clarity, serenity, and peace. It's healthy to take a moment to "zoom out" and notice the wonders around you rather than being so consumed with what's going on internally. Sometimes we just need to take a step back and be observers.

Human beings are all connected, and as much as we'd like to think of ourselves as completely independent, we need each other. We need one another to feel a part of something, to love and to be loved, to learn from, and to be inspired by.

In my favorite sitcom, *Friends*, I love the episode where Phoebe and Joey are arguing over whether a selfless good deed even exists. Joey's argument is that every good deed is not completely selfless because the motivation to serve others is to make us feel good. Basically, Joey is saying that doing good is more about us than we realize.[1]

In Phoebe's humorous attempt to prove Joey wrong, she decides to let a bee sting her so that the bee can look tough in front of his bee friends. She insists that this is a selfless good deed because she was *not* happy about it.

I love their humor around our natural human tendencies. It's true that we are motivated to do good because it fills our hearts with love. Love is what drives us. All we really want in this life is LOVE; we simply get confused about which source to derive it from.

Instead of waiting around for others to love you, be the kind of person who fiercely loves others—someone whose only motivation is to give love freely, unconditionally, and without judgment.

In marriage, we tend to make it all about us. We think thoughts like *What am I getting out of this relationship? I'm always doing more. Why don't I get any appreciation or recognition for all that I do?*

Stop Keeping Score on Who's Doing More

Oh, the score keeping. Let me tell you how effective it's been in our marriage when we keep score on who does more. The times I'm feeling overwhelmed, sleep-deprived, and exhausted are when I start tallying up everything I do and docking Sean points for things he doesn't do. I become consumed with anger and resentment, and I so quickly forget all he contributes to our livelihood.

Basically, what I'm saying is you do *so* much, but you've got to get over yourself. Actually, I'm saying that to me. I need regular doses of humility. Anytime I'm focused more on myself and only noticing everything I contribute to the family, a downward spiral of negativity begins and easily saturates my outlook.

When I take people's actions personally and make them mean something about me, I'm left feeling angry or saddened. For example, maybe I text a friend and she doesn't respond for a few days. Immediately my mind wants to go to thoughts like, *I wonder why she's mad at me. Did I say something to offend her?* I'll even go back and read my previous text messages, trying to find clues as to why she's not texting me back. I can't tell you how many times this and other similar situations have happened to me. I read into things far too often and always end up making them about me in a damaging kind of way.

Usually what ends up happening in those situations is I discover the reason my friend didn't respond right away was because of a life event or something else completely reasonable. Maybe the friend was driving when she read the text and forgot to respond once she was home; maybe she was out of town, her kids were sick, or she responded in her head but forgot to actually respond. I can't tell you how many times I've done this.

The first step to shifting our thinking around this is to be aware. Awareness of our thoughts is the key to all our struggles. Notice the thoughts you are having about the situation without judgment. Allow the thoughts to come through, and simply ask with curiosity, *Is this true?*

As Byron Katie always asks, "Can you absolutely know that it's true?"[2] Most often, the answer will be no. Then she advises us to imagine how we would feel without that thought. Once you isolate the thought and realize it is the cause of your suffering, you can choose to drop the thought. *Unless, of course, you want to keep feeling bad.*

By doing this exercise, you will discover the root cause of your suffering, and at that point you have the power to change how you are feeling about the situation by carefully choosing better thoughts.

I've been practicing this technique for over a year now. I always knew that we have a choice to feel good, but I never really had the desire to choose good thoughts. For some reason, I wanted to sit and ferment with the negativity my mind was offering me; it seemed too difficult to choose better thoughts in the midst of anger or sadness. But as I've been making a conscious effort to work on this, I began to see huge changes in myself and my overall well-being.

I also learned that as you make this practice a daily priority, it gets easier and actually becomes a habit. The result is not only feeling more peaceful in all aspects of your life, but also operating at a much higher frequency, which then opens you up to receiving incredible opportunities.

You only attract what you are putting off, so if you are putting off joy and abundance, you will attract joy and abundance. If you are putting off anger and sadness, naturally you will attract more of that, too.

I saw the effects of my negative thoughts and how they were trapping me in a never-ending cycle. For a while, I couldn't understand why negativity kept showing up in my life. I didn't make the connection that it was my own thoughts and my knee-jerk reaction to take everything personally. When I learned about thought work, everything suddenly became so clear and I realized what was happening.

Since I started practicing thought work, I've been able to see the fruits of my labors. I continue to work hard at managing my thoughts, and the payoff is incredible. Not only do I feel good most of the time, but all the opportunities I'd been hoping for all these years are finally becoming a reality. It's pretty cool to watch things unfold as I make a conscious effort to stay in alignment with the feel-good state of being.

Remember, the goal is to practice awareness without judgment. Simply allow the thoughts, and then choose the ones that make you feel the way you want to feel. You have the power to feel good at any given moment. Now go and make your life about loving others, and be more compassionate with yourself in your efforts to change your thoughts. It takes time and effort, but the payoff is worth it.

Notes

1. *Friends*, "The One Where Phoebe Hates PBS," directed by Shelley Jensen, aired Oct. 18, 1994.
2. Byron Katie, *Loving What Is* (New York: Harmony Books, 2002), 25.

Chapter 11

Why Doesn't Everyone Like Me?

Did you ever think back in high school that your adult self would still be dealing with feelings of being left out or not being part of the "popular" crowd? I sure didn't. However, we all have a deep desire to fit in, to have friends, to be liked, and to be validated, and those desires can sometimes create high school–like feelings even years later.

Ever since I can remember, I've been determined to make sure everyone liked me. This caused me to feel a lot of regret anytime I ever did or said anything that people disagreed with. I was paralyzed by my own unrealistic goal.

It's been surprisingly difficult to accept the fact that not everyone is going to like me. I've spent way too much energy trying to be liked by all, only to discover it's an impossible feat. I can't force people to like me, nor can I force myself to like certain people. We all have our "peeps," the ones we mesh with, and the ones we don't.

Throughout grade school and high school there were those who were recognized as the most "popular," and for some reason I really wanted their approval. As we get older, we continue to identify the "popular kids" in every community—in our neighborhood, workplace, church, and, yes, even within the blogosphere. I'd like to say I left behind my desire to be part of the popular crowd as I moved into adulthood, but the truth is I still found myself being consumed with wanting their acceptance. Now looking back, I shudder at the thought of my desperation.

When I became so laser-focused on getting certain people to like me when clearly they had no interest in being friends, suddenly I was wallowing in self-pity. This feeling was fed with thoughts like *Nobody likes me*, and *Everybody hates me; guess I'll go eat worms.* I would quickly forget about all the wonderful friends I *do* have.

> Get booted from the tribe and start, or find, another tribe that's more your style. You could not only wind up doing what you love surrounded by people you adore who you actually relate to, but you might one day realize you can no longer remember the names of the people whose approval you so desperately thought you would die without.
>
> —Jen Sincero[1]

In the past, I've been guilty of being overly concerned with who followed me on Instagram and who unfollowed me and wondering why particular people wouldn't follow me back. As I began putting so much value on the number of followers or likes I had and allowing it to define and validate who I was, I realized it was time to take a break from social media. It had become a distraction and was keeping me from fulfilling my purpose by causing me to question my importance and lovability and hindering me from believing in my mission and living out my potential.

Each time I take some time away from social media, I always come back feeling empowered and renewed. Sometimes you just need to step away from it all and meditate on all the positive in your life.

We all want to be loved, and too often we mistake love from others as love from the most important sources—God and *you*. We put too much energy into trying to achieve the impossible quest, *becoming the most likeable person in the universe.* Instead, realize we are unconditionally loved *by* the universe.

Not only did I suffer more by seeking love outside God and myself, but also there was no room for becoming the person I really WANTED to be. I was overly focused on being the person everyone else wanted me to be—and that, my friend, is *no* place to be. I felt as though I needed to live up to a certain standard, and by placing this kind of pressure on myself I had a hard time accepting my flaws and allowing for imperfection. I wanted to be amazing, someone that others looked up to, and someone who was admired by many.

When Sean and I first met, it was rainbows and butterflies, unicorns and glitter. He made me feel as though I were the most amazing and perfect woman he'd ever set eyes on. My ego was on cloud nine and my heart was overflowing. I wanted to *always* remain that "perfect woman" in his eyes.

I remember the first time we had an argument as a couple. I felt ashamed, as if I were exposed and no longer the perfect woman to Sean. He'd discovered my dark side. *I sure fooled him.* Thankfully, I came down out of the clouds and understood the fact that being lovable doesn't mean *only if you're perfect.*

Then there was the time when my adult self didn't get invited to an awesome party. I was devastated and fuming with resentment. My brain instantly wanted to make up a story to explain this madness: *They must not like me. Maybe it's something I said. What DID I say the last time I was with those girls? Maybe I'm just not memorable or an enjoyable person to be around.* The brain likes answers, and it instantly goes to its default settings—which are usually negative—to find them. Negative thoughts are much easier for the brain to believe. The positive ones take effort, and rarely do we put forth the effort into creating those positive thoughts.

So you didn't get invited to the party, the girls' night, the baby shower, the wedding, or the fancy event. Does that really mean you're not a lovable person? *Sometimes we act like it.*

Why do we sometimes feel this way when we didn't get the invite? Why do we allow ONE thing to be the evidence of our true self-worth? It's all because of our thoughts and the story we are telling ourselves. Your imagination is really good at creating fictional stories. Get good at asking yourself, "Is this true?"

When I began blogging nine years ago, it started out amazing. People were so supportive and loving of all the content I shared. Until, inevitably, the "haters" began to show up. At first it was difficult to receive negative feedback, but over time I've learned not take their comments personally. Usually the haters hate because they hate something about themselves.

My favorite quote by Joel Osteen:

> Many people let negative words or other people's opinions totally ruin their lives. They live to please other people and honestly think that they can be happy by trying to keep everyone else happy. They don't want anybody to say a negative word about them.
>
> That's simply impossible. You have to accept that not everybody is going to like you, not everybody is going to accept you, and you certainly cannot keep everybody happy. Some people will find fault no matter what you do.[2]

It's human nature to want love and acceptance, but we can't win them all. "You may be the ripest, juiciest peach in the world, but there will always be someone who hates peaches."[3]

Here's a metaphor I came up with based on a humorous life experience I had. It took place back in 2003 when I was serving my Christian service in Germany:

It was a beautiful day in Gera, Deutschland. My colleague and I were sitting outside our church building. We had scheduled an appointment to meet with one of our investigators. We perched down under a tree as we waited for our new friend to arrive. As we began conversing with one another, I saw something that startled me, and I immediately sprung to my feet, stopping her mid-sentence while I frantically brushed my clothes off, flailing my arms, and whipping my hair around.

"What is it?!" she shouted.

As soon as I had a moment to calm down I yelled, "THERE'S A BUG ON YOU!"

This is a classic parallel of taking things personally. The bug was on her, but I was spazzing out, instantly making it all about me.

One thing I learned is that when someone wants to point the finger and claim you have a "bug" on you, it's only because of fear that they, too, have a bug. It's not about you at all.

Allow others to have their opinions of you without taking it personally. This will create a more neutral approach to your self-confidence. You'll get better at finding approval and confidence from within, not always looking for outside acceptance to give you the validation needed in order to keep showing up as your most authentic self. It's time to step into emotional adulthood.

When people don't like us, the only time it becomes a problem is when we make it mean something negative about us. I've gotten really good at asking myself, *What am I making this mean?* By asking this question, I'm usually able to discover why a situation or comment is upsetting me so much. Once I know why I'm reacting the way I am, I can switch my thoughts to be more positive, neutral, and useful. By so doing, I release myself from resentment, frustration, and anger.

It's interesting how when you finally release the desperation of being liked by someone, they often begin to notice you. I remember this happening multiple times with different boys I liked in high school. For a short while, I would act like a little puppy, desperate to get the boy's attention. Eventually I got over him and moved on. Almost every time this happened, the boy actually started paying attention to me, and at that point I literally had no attraction to him anymore. The moment had passed, and by then I simply saw them as little brothers and couldn't even force myself to like them in that way. I remember always saying, "Why NOW?"

As I've become more aware of the thoughts that drive my actions, I've realized I was holding myself back in certain areas of my life. I had the disease to please, and as a result I never spoke up, was never too political, always tried to say just the right thing in order to avoid any opposing feedback, and so on. I knew I needed to make some changes. The more authentic I became, the more I began building my true tribe. Sure, people disagree and unfollow me, but I'm okay with that. I simply take such actions as signs that I'm becoming more of who I am meant to be and creating a stronger connection with the people who really relate to me and are interested in what I have to say.

When I made the decision to detach myself from organized religion, I realized how much I feared other people's judgments. I was afraid to speak out and go public with it. I didn't feel obligated or forced to share it, but I felt it was something I could not keep silent about. Any time you choose to speak your truth on such controversial topics, you better believe the negative feedback, judgment, and anger is bound to follow. I knew this, but it doesn't make it any easier once you're faced with the reality of it. I had people shaming me for opening up about such things, telling me I could be the cause of people doubting their own religion. At first, I felt bad, thinking maybe I WAS hurting people. But that was the old me, the me that was afraid to ruffle any feathers and was easily controlled by the opinions of others.

I realized that I am not responsible for other people doubting their beliefs based on what I choose to share. Not only is it impossible for me to control what people do, but I was confident my message was one of a positive nature. I wanted to help people become more open-minded about religion in general. In religion we all tend to think we are the ONLY ones with the truth, which only breeds judgment and separation. What I came to understand is that we CAN all be right—right for ourselves, but not right for the entire world. We have to allow others to make their own choices, knowing how uniquely we each see the world. I knew I could help many people experiencing a faith crisis. My faith crisis is what led to my spiritual awakening. And how could I not share something that has had such a profound impact on me?

I wonder why people tend to take it so hard when it comes to others' life choices. It IS possible for us to coexist peacefully in a world with such diversity in beliefs. We need NOT take things personally. If we could approach our differences with curiosity rather than judgment, then we might just learn something.

Recently I heard the fable of six blind men and the elephant. It's the perfect analogy when faced with differences of opinions.

Here is John Godfrey Saxe's (1816–1887) version of the story:

The Blind Men and the Elephant

It was six men of Indostan,
To learning much inclined,
Who went to see the Elephant
(Though all of them were blind),
That each by observation
Might satisfy his mind.

The *First* approached the Elephant,
And happening to fall
Against his broad and sturdy side,
At once began to bawl:
"God bless me!—but the Elephant
Is very like a wall!"

The *Second*, feeling of the tusk,
Cried: "Ho!—what have we here
So very round and smooth and sharp?
To me 'tis mighty clear
This wonder of an Elephant
Is very like a spear!"

The *Third* approached the animal,
And happening to take
The squirming trunk within his hands,
Thus boldly up and spake:
"I see," quoth he, "the Elephant
Is very like a snake!"

The *Fourth* reached out his eager hand,
And felt about the knee.
"What most this wondrous beast is like
Is mighty plain," quoth he;
"'Tis clear enough the Elephant
Is very like a tree!"

The *Fifth*, who chanced to touch the ear,
Said: "E'en the blindest man
Can tell what this resembles most;
Deny the fact who can,
This marvel of an Elephant
Is very like a fan!"

The *Sixth* no sooner had begun
About the beast to grope,
Than, seizing on the swinging tail
That fell within his scope,
"I see," quoth he, "the Elephant

Is very like a rope!"

And so these men of Indostan
Disputed loud and long,
Each in his own opinion
Exceeding stiff and strong,
Though each was partly in the right,
And all were in the wrong!

MORAL
So, oft in theologic wars
The disputants, I ween,
Rail on in utter ignorance
Of what each other mean,
And prate about an Elephant
Not one of them has seen![4]

Acceptance, open-mindedness, and love are all we need when discussing such controversial topics. We create our own realities based on our thoughts and our beliefs. My message is simply to remind you of the choice you have to believe whatever it is that brings you peace. Your beliefs don't have to align with anybody else's, nor do they have to perfectly align with any organized religion you may belong to. I simply want people to know they have the choice to use their intuition to guide them in their lives. Choose thoughts and beliefs that resonate with you, empower you, and allow you to feel an abundance of love toward yourself and others.

Sean always reminds me of a quote often attributed to Winston Churchill: "You have enemies? Good. That means you've stood up for something, sometime in your life."

Sean has always been such a good example to me of being his authentic self. I used to hate how honest and vocal he was. I'd be so embarrassed by his outspoken opinions at times, always telling him to tone it down. I was so afraid of offending anyone. But his example has really opened up my eyes. Yes, he has some haters, but he doesn't let that bother him. He chooses to focus on all the people that love and appreciate what he stands for.

As the wise Taylor Swift once said, "The haters gonna hate, hate, hate, hate, hate. Baby, I'm just gonna shake, shake, shake, shake, shake. I shake it off, I shake it off!"[5]

Not everyone is going to like you, and that's totally okay. It doesn't make you any less lovable in the eyes of God. Just keep being you. Speak your truth without any thought of what others will think. Stay connected to the source of true love, and be that beacon of light. Keep showing up, giving your all, loving hard, and building others up even when some try to tear you down.

Notes

1. Jen Sincero, *You Are a Badass* (Philadelphia: Running Press, 2013), 65.
2. Joel Osteen, *Become a Better You: 7 Keys to Improving Your Life Every Day* (New York: Howard Books, 2007), 233.
3. Attributed to Dita Von Teese.
4. *The Poems of John Godfrey Saxe*, Highgate Edition (Boston: James R. Osgood and Company, 1873), 259–61.
5. Taylor Swift, "Shake It Off," *1989*, Kobalt Music Publishing Ltd., 2014.

Chapter 12

My Marriage, My Muse

I wanted to begin this chapter by giving Sean the honors of telling the story of how we met.

Take it away, Sean . . .

Sean

The first time I met Crystal was actually my sophomore year of high school. I was hanging out with some friends, one of whom happened to be Crystal's best friend. I remember seeing this beautiful girl heading out the door with a guy. I thought, *Oh man, that girl is so hot! Too bad she's leaving with some lucky guy.* I know that sounds pretty shallow, but keep in mind I was sixteen at the time. I was briefly introduced to Crystal, but she seemed to be in a hurry, so I didn't get to know her then. I never forgot her face, though. It's like it was permanently imprinted in my mind. I hoped that at some point in the near future I would bump into her again, but that opportunity never really came. I know I probably could have asked her friend to set me up or something, but I actually remember thinking, *She's probably out of my league.*

Fast forward seven years. I had been home from my Christian mission for about two and a half years. Within that period of time I ended up getting married, only to divorce five months later. It was an extremely difficult time for me, but I learned a great deal from that one big mistake.

Eventually I began dating again, keeping my options open, trying to be picky, and making sure I knew exactly what I wanted in a spouse this time. I was burned out, truthfully. The dating scene seemed brutal; not many girls really fit what I was looking for. Of course, I wanted there to be a physical attraction, but I also wanted a girl who was down-to-earth and spiritual. I know I was asking a lot. That combination seemed to be scarce as I was playing the dating game. I went on *so* many first dates. I figured, *Why would I go out with them again and waste their time and mine if the spark isn't there or if I sense something is off?*

It was April 23, 2004. I was on a date with a girl that one of my best friends set me up with. I had been out with this girl once before and didn't see it going anywhere, but my friend convinced me to just hang out because I wasn't doing anything else. So we were at my house when my phone rang. When I answered, it was my friend way back from ninth grade—aka Crystal's best friend. She explained she was in town from San Diego and wanted to drop by and say hello with a couple of her girlfriends. I was excited to reconnect since I hadn't seen her since high school. When they arrived, I instantly recognized Crystal. Needless to say, I was pretty excited.

We visited at my house for a while, and I discovered that Crystal was single, that she was working in my industry of network marketing, and that she too had served a Christian mission. In fact, I remember when they told me Crystal just got home from her mission in Germany, my response was, "You were a missionary?!" All of the girls erupted in laughter because I was so shocked, and of course they could tell how much I admired her service.

We had been visiting for about thirty minutes when my date, my best friend, and my best friend's date decided they had seen enough. They said to me, "Hey, we're gonna head out, and you can just meet up with us when you are done here, okay?"

I felt like a jerk, but I couldn't pass up this opportunity to get to know Crystal better.

The girls stayed a while longer. As they were walking out of my driveway to leave, I wanted to make sure this wouldn't be the last time I would see my dream girl, so I asked Crystal for her number, and she gave it to me.

When they drove off, I felt like I had just won the lottery! I was so glad that I took that call. I also had an amazing feeling, and I knew that God had just sent Crystal to my doorstep. I also knew I was going to marry this girl.

In fact, that night I called my friend Garrett, the one who had set me up with my original date, and said something like, "Dude, could you believe Crystal?"

His response was, "I know! You are going to marry that girl."

I countered, "I know; I knew it right away too!"

Sure enough, it was meant to be. Within a matter of three dates or so, Crystal and I were talking about our future plans to get married. It felt so right, more right than anything I had ever done in my life. We were married three months later.

What can I say other than I am so grateful that God is in charge? I am so happy and can't imagine my life without Crystal in it. Now we have four unbelievable children together, and it just really sends things over the top for me. When I look in their eyes, I simply know, just like I did the day I met Crystal, that it was all meant to be.

Crystal

Aw, he makes me melt like an ice pop on the fourth of July.

Yes, it sounds like a beautiful blissful fairytale. But I'm here to tell you that even fairytales have their struggles.

To be honest, my relationship with Sean has been extremely passionate in every sense of the word. In love and anger, attraction and rage. The intense emotions that I've experienced in our marriage are undeniably my inspiration for many a blog post. Not only does our marriage teach me priceless life lessons, but also Sean himself teaches and inspires me every day.

He's made me aware of my weaknesses and my strengths. He's taught me, by example, how to be more assertive and adapt leadership qualities; how to be confident and humble simultaneously; how to research, read instructions, and read reviews. *I hate all of that.* As I watch him roll around on the floor playing with our children, I'm reminded of the importance of cherishing the present moment. I see his passion for the outdoors, and it prompts me to take a look around and relish in nature.

Sean is the most selfless person I've ever met; he's always willing to drop everything to help me or the kids. There's not much he's not willing to do for us. Watching him clean the shower drain just does something for me. The way he dry heaves while removing the nasty hair buildup . . . I don't know what it is, but he's never looked hotter.

He's MOSTLY willing to listen to me ramble about my feelings for hours on end. Seriously, any man that has the patience to LISTEN to a woman talk about her feelings is a saint in my eyes. He makes all the Costco runs, plans our vacations, handles our finances and insurance, pays the bills, and does the taxes. He's the one signing the kids up for sports, taking them to practices and games, and running around town finding them the equipment they need. He's always willing to help with the laundry and the dishes, wiping bums, and wiping noses. He's good at making meals, making memories, and making me laugh.

Our marriage has been the source of most of my growth over the past fourteen years. I've often wondered how something can be so amazing yet so exasperating all at the same time. One moment I can't stand living with the man, and the next I feel I could literally die without him. It's a mystery how I could be so angry with him but then seconds later feel so much love and adoration I just want to melt into his arms and shower him with my unending love . . . or at least until he says or does something to make me mad.

Am I just crazy? Or is this the real definition of marriage?

I remember there were many times, mostly when I was up all night tending to a newborn or stuck at home with a baby while the rest of the family went out for an adventure, that I would wallow in self-pity, thinking of how much more I do than Sean. It's easy to focus on all the things your spouse doesn't do when you're sleep-deprived and overwhelmed with the constant tending to others' needs while yours are put on hold for a season.

Because of my anger and resentment at times, I've collected a nice sum of humorous stories. We both laugh now looking back at some of the things I've done in reaction to my frustration toward him. Like the time I "unfriended" him on Facebook. As if that really meant something big. *A warning to you all, do NOT upset me, or you just might be unfriended too.*

Here's another funny story. We were on a date, about to go into a movie, when Sean said something that totally offended me. I was so angry that I yelled "I'm walking home," along with a couple swear words, I believe. He went into the theater to get a rain check for our movie tickets, and while he was doing that I began a game of hide and seek. I was too far from home to actually walk, and I knew Sean would come looking for me.

So I began walking through buildings, thinking I would challenge Sean's seeking skills a bit. I was wearing heels, and I hadn't made it far before I felt blisters forming. I found a shady spot under a tree, sat down, and waited for Sean to find me. Before long, I saw Sean pull up in a nearby parking lot. As he made his way toward me, I could see the look on his face. With a little smirk he began quoting *Nacho Libre*:

"'How did you find me?' . . . 'I saw you from the village.'"[1]

If you haven't seen that movie, then seriously, go watch it, and you will die laughing. I was so mad at the time, trying hard to hold a straight face. But when he said this, I couldn't hold back the laughter. Sean has a way of making light of situations and finding the humor in our arguments—something I truly appreciate. He helps me relax and reminds me not to take life so seriously.

Every time we go through a rough patch in our marriage, we always grow closer and learn valuable lessons from it. Coming from a woman of *many* years in age, and over a decade of marriage experience, here are a few little nuggets of advice.

1. Stop Talking.

No, I'm kidding—*but not really.* What I mean is to stop including your husband in your overanalyzation of feelings and emotions. As much as I want my husband to replace my "BFF," it just isn't going to happen. Sure, my husband is my best friend, but not the kind of "bestie" friendship you had in high school. Am I right? You know, the one you'd spend hours on the phone with, who you stayed awake ALL night with chatting it up, literally just TALKING about anything and everything? Women simply never tire of conversing—*should I really be using the word "simple" in the same sentence describing women? Face it: we're complex.*

Talking is our favorite hobby. Men like sports, and we like a nice long chat. Women like to talk about life, and men just like to live it. They don't need to analyze their thoughts, social situations, and what their purpose is. They just live, and that's enough for them. I'm kind of jealous of their natural zen approach to life.

I still find myself getting annoyed when Sean isn't in the mood to talk about *everything*, or if he doesn't say just the right thing. I forget he's a MAN, not a woman, and ultimately, I prefer it that way.

We just need to learn to tone it down a bit and save the loooooong talks for our gal pals. If you don't have girl friends to talk to, then call your mom or your sister, or just get out in public. It's surprisingly easy to find another woman to talk to. I do it all the time when I'm at the park with my kids. It's awesome!

One of the reasons I created my Wannabe Balanced event is to bring like-minded women together for that girl time we all need and crave; to make new friends and build long-lasting friendships.

2. Stop Bringing Up Old Fights.

This one is actually REALLY tough for me, and maybe for most women. We don't let go of things very easily, do we? Even though Sean has apologized for things he's said or done in the past, I find myself repeatedly bringing up old stuff.

This definitely doesn't improve your relationship with your husband. We can't move forward while looking backward. We have to "let it go, let it go!"[2]

3. Stop Trying to Be Right.

We have had many disagreements over the years. How could we not? We are two different people, with two different backgrounds, personalities, and opinions. I've learned that it's more important to keep the peace in our home than it is to force my opinion on Sean.

Focus more on what you *do* agree on. We need to remember the things that brought us together in the beginning. It's funny how when we're first dating we so easily see the good in one another and the things we have in common. Then somehow as the years go on, we get a little too comfortable noticing and voicing the things we do *not* like about each other, which then leads to the urge to try and change them.

We will have disagreements in marriage; we just need to learn how to agree to disagree. We need to try to see things through their point of view.

> Real love is unconditional. Real love accepts the perfection of all . . . accepts that EVERYTHING is perfect just the way it is, and EVERYONE is perfect just the way they are! When we accept everything and everyone just the way they are, there is no reason to find fault or judge. When we are able to accept the perfection in everything and everyone, the ego doesn't get bogged down with its fears—fear of not being equal, fear of being rejected, fear of not being good enough, fear of failure, fear of success, fear of the future, fear of being unworthy, or whatever the fears may be. The problem is too many of us are so emotionally involved in trying to get others to change that we fail to realize that the only person we can change is OURSELVES!
>
> —Karol K. Truman[3]

Sean and I are getting better at allowing one another to be who we want to be instead of trying to fit each other into a mold. I've noticed a huge shift in our marriage since both Sean and I have adapted more acceptance toward one another. As I've learned to let go of controlling the way Sean thinks and acts, I've discovered a new appreciation for him. I'm able to see the things that used to irritate me in a new light. No longer do I allow them to affect me; they simply are what they are, and I don't expect anything different. I've gained a new appreciation for everything Sean does. I can literally put myself in his shoes and look at things through his eyes.

Our new approach to adapt more acceptance in our marriage has rendered less judgment overall. It's a much happier way to live.

> When you judge another, you do not define them; you define yourself.
>
> —Wayne W. Dyer[4]

I've realized that my judgments toward Sean were simply a reflection of the judgments I placed on myself. We all want to be met with understanding and compassion, and my judgments toward Sean were keeping me from having compassion toward myself. They only placed more pressure on me to be perfect.

Judgment separates us from each other and categorizes one partner as being better than the other. It directly contradicts our ultimate goal in marriage, which is to become one. Life is a classroom; not a test. Learning is the goal, and the best way to learn is through experience. So let's allow our spouses to experience life, make their own choices, and learn the lessons they need and want to learn.

Overall, I think that laughter has been the most valuable component in our marriage. One thing that drew me to Sean initially was his sense of humor. When you can loosen up and laugh at your mistakes, it changes everything. It instantly lifts your mood and reminds you that this life is all about learning and experiencing. It's also about finding joy, and there is true joy in laughter. It's my favorite thing to do, and I am so grateful for

Sean's determination to make me laugh even when I'm trying so hard to stay angry.

Notes

1. *Nacho Libre*, directed by Jared Hess (Hollywood, CA: Paramount Pictures, 2006), DVD.
2. *Frozen*, directed by Chris Buck and Jennifer Lee (Burbank, CA: Walt Disney Pictures, 2013), DVD.
3. Karol K. Truman, *Feelings Buried Alive Never Die*, rev. ed. (St. George, UT: Olympus Distributing, 2003), 50.
4. *The Power of Intention* (Hay House Inc., 2004).

Chapter 13

Why Doesn't He Support My Dreams?

> You just can't turn tricks forever. You gotta have a goal. Do you have a goal?
>
> —Kit DeLuca, *Pretty Woman*[1]

When we set out to change our lives or reach big goals, we begin with a lot of determination and excitement. We go "all in" and do everything we know how to do—only to find out it is much harder than we anticipated. Maybe we don't see the results we want, or our efforts just flat-out aren't working. This causes us to think thoughts like *Maybe I'm just no good at this.*

This is the most difficult phase to get past, because our mind wants to resist doing anything new or challenging. Our brains like familiarity and efficiency—in other words, taking the path of least resistance. When things get hard, we tend to rely on other people to encourage us.

We all need cheerleaders to lift us out of our slumps, but sometimes they are nowhere to be found. The ones we thought were supposed to be our biggest fans—who can give us the boost we need—don't always live up to our expectations. Instead, sometimes people validate our own discouraging thoughts. This is the point where most people give up and quit.

When I first told Sean about my desire to put on an annual Wannabe Balanced event, he wasn't too thrilled about the idea. He knows how much work is involved in organizing an event, and he was worried I'd be all-consumed—that it would require too much of my time. Needless to say, he wasn't my number-one fan when it came to putting on events.

The process of organizing my first event was extremely discouraging because I couldn't find a venue to host it. I remember crying to Sean, telling him how frustrated I was, in hopes he would say all the right things, like "You've got this, Crystal. You'll find a place—don't give up. Everything will work out if you just keep trying."

Instead he said, "Crystal, you know you don't HAVE to do this event. Events are hard; it's not necessary."

I was disappointed in his response because the last thing I wanted him to do was talk me out of it.

We experienced a lot of this kind of thing over the years when I first started blogging. Sean didn't always understand my motivations: WHY I wanted to blog and WHY I wanted it to be successful. He just thought, *We make plenty of money; you don't need to do this.* My aspirations were the cause of a lot of arguing, frustration, and resentment in our marriage. I resented him for not supporting my dreams, and he resented me for the time I was devoting to them.

When I first began blogging, I was full of excitement and enthusiasm about my newfound passion. I wanted Sean to be outwardly expressing the same amount of excitement as me; I thought he should be just as enthused as I was. I mean, why wouldn't he be? I was about to embark on the coolest endeavor of all. I would be writing about our life, airing out our dirty laundry, and publicly sharing intimate details of our marriage. How could he NOT be excited about this?

Not only was he against sharing personal details online, but he also didn't like the sudden diversion of my time. I was busier than I was before, and I was definitely more distracted and focused on things that didn't make sense to him.

I was open to his concerns, but I also made his lack of understanding mean I was failing as a wife and a mother. I was overwhelmed with guilt for even having the desire to blog. I wondered what was wrong with me. Why couldn't I just be content being a mother? I must be a horrible, selfish person for having passions outside of motherhood.

I felt like I needed to suppress my desires to write, share, and create. I wanted more than anything to be the perfect wife and mother and to live up to every expectation he had of me. I wanted to please him and make him happy. I also wanted to please others and prove that I was worthy of being a mother. However, the more I tried to suppress my desires, the more conflicted I felt. I couldn't pinpoint the cause of my discontentment at first, but over time it became increasingly evident that self-expression was essential for my own peace and happiness.

I held on to a lot of resentment toward Sean in those early blogging years, even though he never intended to hurt my feelings or kill my enthusiasm. Thankfully, both of us are now able to look back at that season of our marriage and clearly understand the issue. Neither of us was at fault; it was just a learning curve. We both needed time to figure out how to come together with understanding and support.

Initially, I wanted him to see things the way I did. I wanted him to be excited about the same things I was excited about, and I wanted him to *say* everything I needed to hear. I learned that I needed to be less needy and allow him to feel and express his concerns.

Sean learned that pursuing goals and learning new skills is something I absolutely need and crave. He knows that repressing my inclinations to pursue different things only makes for an unhappy and unfulfilled mama. And when mama ain't happy, ain't nobody happy.

What I've come to realize through experience is that the ones you love the most won't necessarily be your support at times. First and foremost, you have to believe in yourself. I constantly remind myself that the only person who can meet my needs is me.

Blogging wasn't the only big life decision I ever made while feeling unsupported. When I got married, my best friend didn't support it. She and Sean didn't really get along, which is funny because she's the one who actually introduced me to him.

Have you ever researched personalities? It turns out their personalities are very similar, and people with similar personalities tend to either love or hate each other. My best friend and Sean definitely weren't fond of one another. They were great friends before Sean and I got together, but the dynamics changed once I became Sean's wife.

It was a very difficult time for me. I was in the midst of one of the best seasons of marriage—while at the same time losing my best friend. As I mentioned in chapter five, change is often described as feeling the emotions of death and birth simultaneously—the death of your old life and the birth of a new one.

I don't have any hard feelings toward my long-lost BFF. I will cherish our memories for the rest of my life. I've mourned the loss of our life together as young teenage girls, flirting our way into dance clubs and free meals, staying out late and meeting up with boys, and experiencing true independence together when we both moved to Arizona right after high school.

The Dixie Chicks song "Wide Open Spaces" is a song that will always remind me of our life in Arizona together.

> Who doesn't know what I'm talking about?
> Who's never left home, who's never struck out
> to find a dream and a life of their own
> a place in the clouds, a foundation of stone . . .
> She needs wide open spaces.
> Room to make her big mistakes.
> She needs new faces . . .

I've come to accept that some friendships have a lifespan. I saw a great quote on Pinterest once. It read:

> Life is like an elevator. Sometimes you
> have to stop and let people off.

We tried for a few years to maintain our friendship, but I think we both got to a point of acceptance. We knew things would no longer be the same and that it was time to move on. The sadness, anger, and frustration I felt toward her is no longer something I possess. It's taken years for me to get to this place, but I'm happy to say now I have so much love in my heart for her. Yes, I miss her, but I miss a lot of things about that age as a young, newly independent woman.

We can't go back in life. We have to keep moving forward and appreciate every season of life. There is so much beauty to be recognized, but it can only be seen if we are focused on the present.

Understand that others don't *need* to understand. They may understand one day, and they may not. In the meantime, I can't hold my breath. I need to have my own back and keep following my own North Star. I can lead my life with love and listen to feedback while at the same time remaining steadfast in what I know is right for me.

Other people's lack of support doesn't mean they don't love us or don't want to see us succeed. It only means they may not see the vision like you do—or they don't want to see you fall on your face or get hurt. It's just as hard for others to accept change in you as it is for you to change. Our brains like things to remain familiar and comfortable.

Finding a teacher or a mentor can also be extremely valuable when trying to pursue difficult goals. It doesn't even have to be someone you work one-on-one with; it could be a podcaster or an author you don't know personally but can learn what they know and how they've succeeded at reaching their goals.

Most importantly, we need to be actively working on our minds—gathering everything that's in our minds and putting it all down on paper, questioning those thoughts, creating believable positive ones, moving forward, and taking action.

Blogging has taught me that the more you put yourself out there, the more you open yourself up for judgment and criticism—which is sometimes enough to keep us from doing it. Most of us fear hearing what other people think and getting any negative feedback. We tend to think that those who are doing a lot of good and spreading positivity receive nothing but love and admiration.

This is definitely not the case. Haters exist, and they are everywhere. They live to tear people down; not because they are bad, awful people, but because hate is what's familiar to them. They don't love themselves and therefore don't know how to love others.

Growing up with tremendous dysfunction within my home, I experienced a lot of shame. One thing I learned that set me free from the shame was to be open about things. The more I shared what my life was *really* like, the more I felt free from the bondage of shame. As I've studied shame a little more, I've learned that the feeling of shame only intensifies when you hide things. Brené Brown often says that shame only needs three things to grow: secrecy, silence, and judgment.

By learning this at such a young age, I became an extremely open person when it comes to my life; I'm not afraid to share how crazy I am.

For instance, I recently sent out an email to my subscriber list, sharing some marriage advice. In the same sentence, I mentioned that I may or may not have scratched Sean once out of anger and rage, drawing blood, during one of our arguments.

I had an unexpected response from one of my subscribers. She was absolutely disgusted with my actions and could *not* believe someone as "crazy" as me would dare give marriage advice.

I honestly think we learn the most from the crazies. Seriously, they've been to the dark side and back. I'm constantly reading books and listening to podcasts by people who were once drug addicts, or struggled with severe depression, or were even homeless at one point. Those are the people who truly inspire me—people who can overcome extreme circumstances and struggles. It's amazing to witness the growth and real change of another person; not only does it allow others to say "me too"; it gives them a glimpse into what is possible for even the craziest of people.

In the past, it's been hard for me to accept when others are unsupportive of me, especially when I try so hard to support others. When I lovingly support someone, it seems only fair that they would return the favor, right? Well, yes! In a perfect world.

But that's completely out of my control. Expectations reduce joy, and *boy, have they reduced mine when I focus too much on how I think others should be doing things.* I've gotten really worked up over the lack of support from certain people, and it has only caused me more pain. I'm learning to be more tolerant and accept that everyone has different circumstances, everyone does things differently, everyone thinks differently, and yes, not everyone is going to like me.

PLUS, I shouldn't be serving and loving others with the expectation of getting something in return . . . My bad . . .

It takes courage to go after your goals and dreams without relying on the support of others. It's great if you get it, but it's important to be in a place of not needing it in your formula for success.

Courage is all you need. Courageously work toward what you feel called to do. Don't listen to the naysayers, and believe in your own ability to succeed, knowing full well that failure is part of success. Pick yourself up and try again, and again, and again.

Note

1. *Pretty Woman*, directed by Garry Marshall (Burbank, CA: Touchstone Pictures, 1990), DVD.

Chapter 14

Feeling Beautiful at Any Age, Shape, or Size

My first experience with pregnancy was everything I hoped for. I gained thirty-five pounds exactly, didn't look pregnant until I was five months along, and gave birth with no complications to a healthy eight-pound baby. As I lay there on the hospital bed while my new baby slept, I lifted my gown to reveal what had become of my former basketball belly. To my surprise, it was flat—*well, at least until I stood up.* Even then, it didn't match the horror stories people had warned me about. Six weeks later, I was wearing my pre-pregnancy jeans and two-piece swimsuits without any signs of ever having been pregnant. I thought I was going to be one of those lucky women that pops them babies out and looks amazing while doing it.

Then baby number two came along and crushed my dreams. I gained fifty pounds and delivered a nine-and-a-half-pound child, leaving me plenty of stretch marks to prove it. When he was six weeks old, I wondered why the pounds weren't just melting away like they had so politely done the first time around.

I seemed to gain a little more weight with each pregnancy and had a much harder time getting it off after delivery. It took me a full year to lose the weight after Owen (my fourth) was born, and there is no way my saggy, shriveled-up midsection will be making an appearance at the pool EVER again.

As each post pregnancy became progressively harder, I learned a few things. Number one, patience is my least favorite virtue. I realized that my first pregnancy set the bar pretty high, and for that reason I continued to beat myself up over how long it took me to lose the weight. I thought I was just not being disciplined enough or that I was being lazy with my workouts, but it seemed that the harder I tried, the more those fat cells were determined to stick around. I would work my butt off at the gym, cutting as many calories as possible while trying to maintain my milk supply. Each week, I would weigh in with not so much as a pound lost. I would cry and complain to Sean that it wasn't fair that men never had to deal with this.

He did his best to comfort me, and never once made me feel less than sexy. He would tell me, "Hey, it took you nine months to gain the weight, don't you think you should allow your body at least that much time, *if not more*, to return to its former state?"

I hated it when he said that. I wanted to prove that patience wasn't part of the equation. I thought as long as I had enough motivation and discipline, I could skip learning the lesson of patience.

So to all you beautiful nursing mamas, or even not nursing mamas trying to lose the baby weight: Can I just tell you? Please be gentle with yourself. You are an amazing vessel that creates life! How cool is that? *Speaking of which, I've often wondered what God was thinking when He decided on the role men would play in the process of procreation.*

In Sean's defense, I guess he does deserve props for taking care of my roller-coaster of emotions throughout pregnancy, postpartum, and one week out of every month of our marriage. I know it must have been hard to deal with all the drama I've created over the years. Dang hormones!

Once I was done having babies and had been back in my size five jeans for a few years, there was yet another thing I had to learn to accept—and that is the fact that I'm aging. I've realized that for my entire life, I've never been completely happy with my looks—whether it be my body, my hair, or my skin. It was always something.

In the past, I spent way too much time worrying about my acne, saggy butt, stretched-out tummy, age spots, fine hair, and fine lines. Now, I'm slowly but surely learning what true beauty really means.

A few years ago, I read this awesome book called *Change It Up*. In the book, Amanda Dickson stated something truly profound:

> The way to feel beautiful at any age, with any body, is to shift the focus. We no longer need people to look at us to feel beautiful—we need to look AT PEOPLE. We become the mirror for them. Beauty, real beauty, truly is in the eyes of the beholder and not the "beheld." The beholder feels beautiful herself because she loves what she beholds. When our toddlers throw their arms up into the air for us to scoop them up, we feel beautiful. When our [husband runs] to greet us after [he returns] home from a trip, we feel beautiful. When our children get married and tell us they're expecting their first child, we feel beautiful. None of those feelings requires that we look any certain way for other people to admire. We can be thin or heavy, wrinkled or smooth, tan or pale, weak or strong. We can "let ourselves go" or stay in perfect shape. We can be exactly the way we are right now at this moment . . . and we can be the way we'll be in five years and twenty years and beyond. We can age without any

> concern for stretching our face until it feels smooth. The feeling of beauty requires only that we look at the objects of our love and devotion.
>
> This is finally it—the end of needing to be seen, and the beginning of seeing.[1]

As time goes on, I'm able to grasp this way of seeing beauty more and more. It's simply switching our focus and being grateful for each moment we have with the ones we love. I truly feel beautiful when I hold my babies, care for them, and love them. It's quite incredible how this method of seeing beauty works—we place less focus on worrying about our aging bodies and more focus on SEEING the beauty in others. At the same time, we're accepting ourselves just the way we are, physically, mentally, and spiritually.

I mentioned in a previous chapter that my son Owen was born with a little ear, which in medical terms is called microtia. We've never talked to him about his cute little ear and have even grown his hair out long so others wouldn't see it and bring it to his attention. We adore his little ear, but of course want to avoid possible hurtful remarks from other kids.

He's now almost five years old, and he had never realized that his one ear is different until recently. Just the other day I was tickling his back, and then I kissed his little ear, as I do often. This time I said, "I love your cute ears." He said, "Mom, do I have a tiny ear?"

I knew this day would eventually come, and I had often wondered what he would think about it once he became aware of the difference.

"Yes, I love your little ear," I replied.

At that moment, he got a big smile on his face, put his hand on his ear, and said, "I love my little ear, too." Then he began to giggle and said, "Little ear, big ear," as he touched both ears.

How amazing is the example of a child! We can learn so much from these carefree little beings, who are so unaware of what others think of them and unapologetically confident in a way that I'm quite envious of.

Since I've embarked on this mission to allow and appreciate the inevitable aging process we all must experience, I've been searching for all kinds of inspiration around the particular topic of aging.

Eckhart Tolle teaches in his book *The Power of Now* that meditation can literally slow down the aging process.[2] As we identify ourselves more by our inner being rather than our outward appearance, we come to realize that we really don't age at all. It takes a lot of practice to comprehend how to adapt this state of mind, but it all comes down to being fully in the present moment, not worrying about past or future, and paying closer attention to how our inner being is not really the body. The body is the vehicle we possess now, but ultimately it is not who we are.

I've also been studying the law of attraction and how it affects self-confidence. How we can learn to accept our "mom bods" and embrace the aging process.

I recently watched the movie *I Feel Pretty*, and it really resonated with me. In the movie, Amy Schumer plays a woman who struggles with low self-esteem and poor body image until one day she hits her head, and suddenly she sees herself as a thin and sexy supermodel. Her confidence skyrockets, she's able to land a cute boyfriend, and she finally gets her dream job. The cool part about it is her appearance didn't actually change—everyone else saw her the same as they always had—it was only her own perception that changed. Since she believed she was beautiful, she became empowered to live her life fearlessly.

The movie shows such a great representation of what is possible for all of us when we change our thoughts and beliefs about the way we look. When we feed our minds with enough positive thoughts about the way we look, the way we look literally changes. We create our realities by what we think, and when we begin to see ourselves as beautiful and sexy, it creates the kind of confidence that can truly change our lives.

Confident people attract people, and great opportunities seem to flock their way. The best part about this is that we all have the choice and ability to BE confident. Successful people aren't confident BECAUSE of their success; they were first confident, and THEN they became successful. We can choose right now to FEEL confident—it all starts with our thoughts. What are you thinking about yourself when you look in the mirror? Are you noticing your beauty, or are you silently comparing yourself to someone else? Wishing you looked different than you actually do? Take a look at yourself again, and this time, relish in your beauty. Look deep into your own eyes and actually SEE yourself. See your non-physical being and remember that is who you truly are. The more you see yourself that way, the more others will see you that way, too.

I love more than anything when I meet someone who in the eyes of the world would be qualified as not pretty, but they are bursting with confidence. I am drawn to them like a fruit fly loves fruit. I can't help but want to be around them. Their energy, charisma, humor, knowledge, and experience—I just want to curl up in their lap and be their little pet.

My new approach to feeling beautiful at any age is to simply be more mindful in everything I do. I'm treating my body with kindness by feeding it healthy foods and getting plenty of exercise and sleep. Speaking of which, I created a meal plan blueprint back when I was nursing and decided to make it available to all my awesome subscribers. Just go to www.wannabebalanced.com/mealplan to get your free download. It's a week's worth of nutrient-dense meals along with a grocery list of items you'll need.

Not only am I making sure to take care of my body, but in addition, my goal and purpose has completely shifted. No longer is eating healthy about changing my appearance; I'm doing it because I love and appreciate my body. I want to take care of it simply because it's done such a good job of taking care of me—my spirit. It allows me to experience so much because of its physical capabilities, and for that I am most grateful.

My daily meditation allows me to get centered and helps me recognize the negative thoughts that tend to pop up from time to time. I simply notice them and assist them on their way out. I also spend a lot of time visualizing. I visualize the way I want to see myself, as beautiful and flawless. Just like in the movie, "I Feel Pretty," I can train my brain to see myself exactly the way I want to see myself. I visualize going about my day with confidence, with no make-up covering up my imperfections and radiating love for others and love for myself. That is the goal.

I believe in the effectiveness of meditation and visualizing. It's extremely powerful, and if you begin making it a daily practice, you, too, will see the shift happening little by little over a long period of time. It's gradual, but it absolutely works.

Notes

1. Amanda Dickson, *Change It Up!* (Salt Lake City: Shadow Mountain, 2009), 79.
2. Eckhart Tolle, *The Power of Now* (Novato, CA: New World Library, 2004).

Chapter 15

Online, Offline, or Somewhere in Between

Oh, Myspace, how I miss thee.

Myspace was where it all began for me. I was a new mom feeling completely isolated from the outside world, and then I discovered this really awesome cyber world, a way to meet new friends and share fun pictures of my family. *Why is it so fun to show off our best pictures?*

Little by little, I realized that social media doesn't always portray what's REAL, only the highlight REEL. At first, I didn't notice this; I just got caught up in all the comparisons. At the same time, I was trying to act as though my own life was just as perfect as everyone else I saw on social media.

During my time on Myspace, I was still very much involved with real-life connections. Social media to me then was a way to meet moms near me and plan regular get-togethers. It was awesome! But over time it became easier to stay home and just communicate with friends behind my keyboard. Myspace led to Facebook, Facebook led to blogging, and blogging led to Instagram. Before I knew it, two years had passed, and I hadn't really planned any outings with friends or even invited people over to my house. It wasn't until one day at church, when I found myself struggling not to feel awkward while having a conversation with an acquaintance, that I recognized something was off. Awkwardness was a new thing for me; I've always been a pretty social person. Moving every six months growing up will kick the shyness right out of you! There I was trying to converse, and feeling extremely self-conscious in the intervals of awkward silence.

Later that day, I tried to figure out what was happening to me. Had I lost my mojo? Did motherhood turn me into a little timid mouse that no longer had anything interesting to say?

Suddenly, everything became clear as day. As Les Brown says, "What you don't use, you lose."[1] That is exactly what happened to me! I had gotten so comfortable staying home and connecting to the internet that I wasn't connecting in real life. I had also become obsessed with "likes" and followers; cyber likes were more important to me than I wish to admit. I wanted to feel important, and for some reason likes and followers made me feel temporarily important. I found myself constantly checking my stats and numbers, and eventually it became so consuming that I began to feel depressed. No longer was I appreciating the real-life love I had right within my own home. No longer was I looking to God or within for love and validation. I was full-on addicted to social media, searching for that next hit of dopamine that I sometimes got when I received good feedback on something I posted.

Now don't get me wrong—it's okay to appreciate love and a sense of community and support online, but when it becomes all-consuming and you find yourself hopping on social media multiple times a day to see how many likes or views you got, you know you have a problem.

Once this became clear to me, I knew there was something I needed to do about it. The first step to overcoming addiction is awareness. I still find myself falling back into the same addictive patterns, but I'm aware and better able to catch myself and make the necessary changes to avoid the constant distraction of the phone.

At first, I wondered if maybe I should disconnect from social media altogether and completely close down my accounts. Ultimately, I decided that would not be the most useful approach and regular phone fasts would suffice.

I know there are still many people who despise social media and refuse to jump on the bandwagon; to me, not embracing social media is the same as not embracing any other form of modern-day technology. Yes, there is a dark side to everything, but the world is evolving, and I feel it's our duty to embrace it and not resist it. There is a lot of good happening, thanks to social media—although I know there is equally as much bad happening. That's simply the way life is. Our job is to learn how to use social media for good and to be vigilant as we navigate our way through the inevitable growth of mankind.

So with regular phone fasts and the awareness of my thoughts, I've been able to find a healthy balance with social media. Remember, your thoughts are what determine your emotions. If after using social media you feel sad or not good enough, then take a look at the thoughts that are making you feel that way. Appreciate the beauty you see on social media without any comparisons.

In my opinion, there is nothing wrong with sharing all your best pictures on social media. I mean, why not? We can all be of the understanding that nobody has a perfect life and simply appreciate the beauty and positivity others are trying to put out there. Let's stop hating and start appreciating. We are all equally as valuable and loved, no matter how big our houses are or how many awesome vacations we take. If we all understood that, then there would be less jealousy and resentment on social media.

The quickest way to shift your brain from the comparison mode is to take out a piece of paper and write down all the good in your own life—all the good about YOU, all the good in your husband, your house, your income, your growth, your body, your children, your neighborhood, and so on. Acknowledge all you've accomplished in your own life and what you've overcome.

Sometimes it may feel like someone else's life is better than your own, but that is simply not true. Every single person in this world is dealing with their own insecurities, self-doubt, emotional pain, and suffering. Negative emotions are inevitable, so don't be angry that others post only their highlight reels; instead, appreciate the delight and positivity it radiates. Do we really want to get on social media and hear everyone complain about how hard their lives are? I admit there is a time and place for that, and it can be refreshing when others are completely vulnerable and raw, but there is a better way to do this—be real in a positive way. Share your struggles, but share once you've overcome them to a point of seeing the lesson within the experience. Recycle your pain; take your mess and turn it into your message!

One way I've been able to use social media for good on many levels is by utilizing the live video feature. When I first became aware of how socially awkward I had become, I decided I was going to push myself out of my comfort zone. I wanted to be challenged in such a way that would allow me to regain my communication skills. I discovered Periscope, a live video-streaming app that was popular for about a year until Facebook recognized the growing trend and pounced on the movement. *They don't just jump on the bandwagon; they BECOME the bandwagon, am I right?*

Anyway, I saw Periscope as a fun way to share the different messages of my heart. Instead of writing them out in blog posts, I wanted to make it more personal by sharing it live on video. Improvisation was a new skill I wanted to master. It's a lot harder to share my message live as opposed to being able to articulate every word in a written blog post, but I saw this as an opportunity to grow and connect even more to my online pals.

The thought of being live and on video made me incredibly nervous. I was actually quite surprised at the amount of fear surrounding something that really shouldn't have been that big of a deal. I viewed this as a way to overcome fear and accumulate more courage. I made a goal to do one live video a day for six months, and I did it. It is so fun to go back now and watch my very first video. I remember how scared and nervous I was; my voice was shaky, my palms were sweaty, and I stumbled over my words. It was embarrassing, but I was willing to be embarrassed in order to become fearlessly confident. I'm not saying I'm now an amazing speaker, but I have become so much better at it. I no longer get nervous; I'm comfortable and calm and more capable of sharing my message in a relaxed way instead of being all in my head, bouncing back and forth between thoughts of "What are they thinking of me?" to my actual message. *It's kind of hard to share a message seamlessly when your brain is playing ping-pong with your thoughts.*

Using live video is a way to show others the REAL you. Not only did I cultivate a skill, I continued to use social media for good by spreading positivity and vulnerability. I believe live video can improve your communication, increase your confidence, and help you overcome fear.

Another thing I've noticed about social media is the importance of growing thicker skin. If you want to be authentically you and share publicly your beliefs and opinions, you have to understand that you are opening yourself up for criticism.

In fact, simply being public on social media as I have been has opened me up to criticism regardless of whether or not I've been brutally honest about what I think. For example, I recently participated in a campaign with a large brand. I created a sponsored video for them to use as an ad on Facebook. As a result, this video reached about a million views. The company paid for it to be seen by many people who didn't know me or had never even heard of my blog, and I was made aware of just how mean people can be. The haters come out of hiding and make themselves known. I began getting comment after comment of different women picking me apart: "Look at her fried hair!" "That product is obviously not working for her—look at her skin." "Why is she promoting health when she bleaches her hair?"

To be honest, this hurt, but not as much as I thought it would. Ten years ago, comments like these would have sent me into a deep depression, and I was so proud to witness how much I've grown in my own confidence. I was able to recognize the comments for what they were and remember that haters only hate others because they hate themselves; it's the only reasonable explanation for their behavior. When you're feeling so much love and appreciation for yourself with all your imperfections, you have no room to hate others. You radiate love! This really allowed me a new perspective on love in general. I finally realized that in order to be a kind and loving person—*what we are all striving for*—we have to first love ourselves. I'm sure you've heard this many times in your life, and so did I, but I just didn't get it. I didn't realize that I was focusing more on how I was treating others than how I was treating myself with my own thoughts, nor did I realize how powerful your interactions with others become once you finally learn to love yourself first. It's only then that you can truly become the loving, thoughtful, generous, and compassionate person you're striving to be. I guess I just always thought that you can't be humble and confident at the same time.

Social media is our new reality. You can take it or leave it, but I suggest you take it. Don't be afraid of it; just set boundaries, use it with purpose, avoid the temptation to compare, love yourself, have regular phone fasts, and most importantly, manage your thoughts.

Note

1. As quoted in Habits of the Wealthy, "Les Brown—What to Do When You Feel Lost (Les Brown Motivation)," September 11, 2017, https://www.youtube.com/watch?v=otiiFhqglAk.

Conclusion

AWAKE

As a young girl I always dreamed of becoming an actress. During the two semesters of college I attended, my goal was to major in theater arts then head out to LA-la land to become a famous actress. Growing up feeling unseen by others triggered this desire to be SEEN by many.

About a year ago I was interviewed to appear on a reality TV show featuring bloggers in Utah. At the time I was beyond excited about the opportunity and daydreamed of what my life would be like after finally getting my "big break" into the world of social media fame. I felt as though things were finally coming together for me and I would once and for all know what it's like to be happy and content with who I am.

After years of desperately trying to prove my worth to myself and to others, I thought that perhaps fame is where true happiness lies. Not even world famous, just a small-scale level of fame as a blogger. You know what I mean: those people who have become Instagram-famous or a YouTube sensation. That's all I wanted—not the Brad Pitt and Angelina Jolie famous, just well known among my niche of mommy bloggers.

Year after year I tried and I failed, and then I tried harder and failed harder. I didn't understand why I couldn't quite grasp the life I THOUGHT I wanted.

Now, looking back, I can see that this past year has pulled and stretched me in more ways that I ever thought possible. Not only did I discover that contentedness was available all along, but also I have awakened from the dream state I had been living in for so long. I had a false sense of reality, and even more so, a false sense of happiness.

I thought my achievements would give me that self-worth I had been searching for. Always trying to prove to others that I had value and potential.

The reality TV show never came to be, but in the meantime I entered into a realization of what I REALLY wanted in my life, and fame had nothing to do with it. In fact, fame is the last thing on my mind these days. I have been awakened to the life I KNOW I want, not the life I THINK I want. The difference between knowing and thinking is the difference between the soul and the mind. The soul knows, and the mind thinks. I've learned what the mind creates cannot be trusted as truth. The mind is extremely creative when making up stories. The goal is to find that deeper connection to your soul in order to control the mind rather than *it* controlling you.

Just like I recognize myself waking up, I believe there are so many others who are experiencing what I am: this new level of consciousness, an enlightened way of seeing their own life. More and more I'm meeting people who are coming to the same realization about knowing what they want in life versus doing what others want. We are collectively waking up and discovering that true happiness has been available all along. We've been suffering and striving when all we really needed to do is relax and open our hearts and our minds to a new way of thinking. We are all evolving into a new and wonderful life of more understanding, unity, and consciousness.

As you embark on your own spiritual awakening, you will notice the shift in your focus. Your life becomes more about others and less about you. Instead of wanting more money, you will want more experience. Your newfound humility will catapult you into a more unified way of seeing the world, as opposed to the us-against-them mentality. You become more understanding, a seeker of truth, and obsessed with being healthy rather than being pretty. Addictions are conquered, and SPIRITUAL is who you are. Mind, body, and soul literally become one, and your purpose becomes clearer than ever before.

Acknowledgments

To my husband, Sean. Thank you for loving me unconditionally and accepting me exactly the way I am. You've stood by me through my worst moments and encouraged me when I needed it most. Thank you for allowing me to follow my dreams and keeping me grounded as I pursued them, always reminding me of what matters most. You are the man of my dreams, and I can't imagine walking this journey with anyone else. You are my soulmate!

To Lily, my firstborn. I will always think of you as my little girl, the one who insisted on sleeping right next to me every night for the first three years of your life and who would only nap as long as I napped with you. You are one strong soul. I love watching you grow into a young woman so beautiful and so very kind to other girls your age. You are a born leader, which is why I believe you joined our family first, to pave the way for your younger siblings.

To Oliver, my creative, determined, and so very considerate Oliver. I can't tell you how much you inspire me as I watch you try new things and never give up. You truly believe in your abilities to do great things, and you go for it, knowing that anything great comes with practice, dedication, and consistency.

My sweet Brooklyn Star, my little sidekick. You are such a delight to be around. Every day you give me your sweet hugs and kisses and never forget to express appreciation. You remind me that love is all we need. Thank you for always being such a great big sister to little Owen. He adores you so much. You radiate love for others and also for animals. It's no wonder our pets love you the most.

And my little baby Owen. Although you are no longer a baby, I will always cherish your baby years. Those were some of the most precious moments in my life. I could never get enough of your scent, your soft baby skin, and your sweet snuggles during the many sleepless nights we endured together. You taught me to appreciate life more fully and to never take things for granted. Your strong will reminds me to NEVER give up, haha.

To my mom and dad for raising me. You loved me, provided for me, and always listened when I needed to talk. You taught me many wonderful life lessons, and I will be eternally grateful.

To my father- and mother-in-law, Tony and Randi Escobar, who have always treated me with acceptance and tremendous love since I joined their family in 2004.

To my sisters, who have always been my biggest fans. Thank you for always loving and supporting me throughout my entire life.

To Caeli Thibeault Fenton for inspiring me to write this book.

To all my friends online and offline who continued to support me through my faith transition.

To the team at Cedar Fort Publishing for all their support and hard work in making this book possible: Kathryn Watkins in sales and acquisitions, Wes Wheeler for the beautiful cover, Jessica Pettit and Nicole Terry for the editing help, and Kaitlin Barwick for keeping the book on track and designing the interiors. Thank you for making this dream of mine come true.

And finally to you, my dear reader. Thank you for taking a chance on this book and for allowing me to share my story with you. I hope to meet you in person one day.

Love,
Crystal Escobar

About the Author

When Crystal Escobar first became a mom, she had a hard time figuring out the balance between being there for her kids and being there for herself. It's the ultimate mom dilemma: "Am I a good mom if I have passions and interests outside of motherhood?" So many women can relate. They feel guilty about doing anything else outside of simply tending to their kids or their spouses, yet so many women today are finding themselves unfulfilled and stagnant in terms of their purpose.

There is an abundance of undiscovered talents just waiting to be shared with the world. Ask any woman what her life's purpose is, and you will undoubtedly hear her respond with a phrase such as "I want to bless other people's lives." Finding your passion and purpose is the spark that can ignite a raging fire of joy and enthusiasm within your life.

Crystal began exploring her own personal quest for purpose and balance in 2010. She learned to embrace her inner "mom-treprenuer" and used the blogging platform as a way to keep a personal journal of sorts. She found the time spent writing and sharing her thoughts with others to be extremely rewarding and even therapeutic. There were times she felt guilty for immersing herself into her work. There were times she felt inadequate and insecure while comparing herself to more established household-name bloggers. There were even times when she considered quitting all together, taking a two-year hiatus at one point.

This is a story of perseverance. Crystal's blog has evolved into more than just an online journal; it has become a mission for her—a mission to create a community of other "wannabe balanced" moms who have the desire to become a better version of themselves in motherhood and business, all while juggling the other demands placed upon them. Crystal has been featured on several television news stations for her unique way of promoting a balanced life incorporating mind, body, and soul.

At the age of twenty-seven, Crystal and her husband, Sean, became the youngest-ever millionaires in Isagenix International, a multibillion-dollar nutrition and wellness company, and they retired by the age of thirty-five. Now they spend their time teaching and mentoring others along the same path, putting on yearly events, podcasting, and sharing their lives on Instagram and YouTube. This power couple continues to offer others valuable insights on how you can make your dreams a reality.

Scan to visit

www.wannabebalanced.com